New Directions for
Higher Education

Betsy O. Barefoot
Jillian L. Kinzie
CO-EDITORS

Enhancing and Expanding Undergraduate Research: A Systems Approach

Mitchell Malachowski
Jeffrey M. Osborn
Kerry K. Karukstis
Elizabeth L. Ambos
EDITORS

Number 169 • Spring 2015
Jossey-Bass
San Francisco

ENHANCING AND EXPANDING UNDERGRADUATE RESEARCH: A SYSTEMS
APPROACH
Mitchell Malachowski, Jeffrey M. Osborn, Kerry K. Karukstis,
Elizabeth L. Ambos
New Directions for Higher Education, no. 169
Betsy O. Barefoot and Jillian L. Kinzie, Co-editors

Microfilm copies of issues and articles are available in 16mm and 35mm,
as well as microfiche in 105mm, through University Microfilms Inc., 300
North Zeeb Road, Ann Arbor, MI 48106-1346.

NEW DIRECTIONS FOR HIGHER EDUCATION (ISSN 0271-0560, electronic ISSN
1536-0741) is part of The Jossey-Bass Higher and Adult Education Series and is published quarterly by Wiley Subscription Services, Inc., A
Wiley Company, at Jossey-Bass, One Montgomery Street, Suite 1200, San
Francisco, CA 94104-4594. Periodicals Postage Paid at San Francisco,
California, and at additional mailing offices. POSTMASTER: Send address
changes to New Directions for Higher Education, Jossey-Bass, One Montgomery Street, Suite 1200, San Francisco, CA 94104-4594.

New Directions for Higher Education is indexed in Current Index to Jour-
nals in Education (ERIC); Higher Education Abstracts.

Individual subscription rate (in USD): $89 per year US/Can/Mex, $113
rest of world; institutional subscription rate: $335 US, $375 Can/Mex,
$409 rest of world. Single copy rate: $29. Electronic only–all regions: $89 individual, $335 institutional; Print & Electronic–US:
$98 individual, $402 institutional; Print & Electronic–Canada/Mexico:
$98 individual, $442 institutional; Print & Electronic–Rest of World:
$122 individual, $476 institutional.

Editorial correspondence should be sent to the Co-editor, Betsy O.
Barefoot, Gardner Institute, Box 72, Brevard, NC 28712.

Cover design: Wiley
Cover Images: © Lava 4 images | Shutterstock

www.josseybass.com

CONTENTS

Editors' Notes

Undergraduate research has been shown to be one of the high-impact practices that lead to substantial impacts on students' cognitive and affective development in college. It addresses much of what we believe is important in education, as undergraduate research helps develop critical thinking skills and problem-solving abilities; it also improves retention, student success, graduation rates, and postgraduation achievement. Although the positive outcomes of undergraduate research are now well documented, its practice is still far from universal. Why is that the case? Some of the reasons are cultural or pedagogical, including undergraduate research not being part of the traditions of some disciplines or it not fitting into the curriculum in obvious ways. Other reasons are more practical, such as the challenges of gathering resources to support this activity or faculty issues including how undergraduate research counts in workload, and the rank and tenure process. And, of course, there needs to be institutional buy-in at a level that allows for the meaningful engagement of all the participants.

Despite the challenges, there are now many success stories from campuses that have institutionalized undergraduate research. We have been involved with many colleges/universities over the years that have moved to a level of undergraduate research that has led to deep and transformative changes in the campus practices and culture. In this volume, many of those success stories are described by the very practitioners who have made them happen. Six state systems and private/public consortia with whom we have worked over the past five years describe their journeys to harness the power of the collectives to foster the institutionalization of undergraduate research at campuses across the systems/consortia. Their experiences highlight many of the issues that others need to consider as they move toward teacher–scholar and student-as-scholar models. Their institutional commitments to undergraduate research have led to enriched curricula and more creative and dynamic learning environments. At the system/consortium level, these strategic efforts have generated opportunities for meaningful cross-campus discussions on curricula and pedagogy, fostered research collaborations among departments and campuses, and enhanced interdisciplinary activities. We discuss the model of change that systems/consortia have used to move to this new paradigm and consider ways to apply these models to other large-scale initiatives. Enjoy.

NEW DIRECTIONS FOR HIGHER EDUCATION, no. 169, Spring 2015   © 2015 Wiley Periodicals, Inc.
Published online in Wiley Online Library (wileyonlinelibrary.com) • DOI: 10.1002/he.20117

This project would not have been possible without the support of the National Science Foundation's Division of Undergraduate Education (NSF-DUE Awards #0920275, #0920286).

Mitchell Malachowski
Jeffrey M. Osborn
Kerry K. Karukstis
Elizabeth L. Ambos
Editors

MITCHELL MALACHOWSKI is a professor of chemistry at the University of San Diego and a coordinator of CUR's Institutionalizing Undergraduate Research Program.

JEFFREY M. OSBORN is the dean of the School of Science and professor of biology at The College of New Jersey, and a coordinator of CUR's Institutionalizing Undergraduate Research Program.

KERRY K. KARUKSTIS is the Ray and Mary Ingwersen Professor and chair of chemistry at Harvey Mudd College, and a coordinator of CUR's Institutionalizing Undergraduate Research Program.

ELIZABETH L. AMBOS is the executive officer of the Council on Undergraduate Research.

1

This chapter reviews the evidence for the effectiveness of undergraduate research as a student, faculty, and institutional success pathway, and provides the context for the Council on Undergraduate Research's support for developing and enhancing undergraduate research in systems and consortia. The chapter also provides brief introductions to each of the chapters in the theme volume.

Realizing Student, Faculty, and Institutional Outcomes at Scale: Institutionalizing Undergraduate Research, Scholarship, and Creative Activity Within Systems and Consortia

Mitchell Malachowski, Jeffrey M. Osborn, Kerry K. Karukstis, Elizabeth L. Ambos

The Transformative Role of Undergraduate Research

Many academicians have embraced undergraduate research (UR) as the pedagogy for the 21st century (Brew, 2010; Lopatto, 2009). The melding of teaching and research into a collaborative enterprise of student and faculty mentor is viewed as an innovative curricular reform that eliminates the historic tension between teaching and scholarship and motivates undergraduates to learn by doing. Recognition of the pedagogical value of UR might be best attributed to numerous rigorous studies of the impact of UR on student learning and personal growth, as well as the wider impact on all other stakeholders of higher education, including faculty, institutions of all types, business and corporate associates, and nonprofit community partners.

UR is a high-impact practice that sparks students' interest in learning and love for the discipline and that improves retention, student success, graduation rates, and postgraduation achievement (Hathaway, Nagda, & Gregerman, 2002; Hu, Scheuch, Schwartz, Gayles, & Li, 2008; Hunter, Laursen, & Seymour, 2006; Kardash, 2000; Kuh, 2008; Kuh, Kinzie,

Schuh, Whitt, & Associates, 2010; Laursen, Hunter, Seymour, Thiry, & Melton, 2010; Laursen, Seymour, & Hunter, 2012; Lopatto, 2009; Osborn & Karukstis, 2009; Seymour, Hunter, Laursen, & DeAntoni, 2004). Research on UR shows compelling benefits of participating in scholarly work for students across demographic groups and disciplines—and even higher gains for women, first-generation, and minority students (Kuh, 2008; Osborn & Karukstis, 2009). Yet, UR opportunities are often optional and highly selective, missing the very students who could benefit most from them.

While the significant benefits from undergraduate engagement in research are clear, the drive to institutionalize UR is perhaps intensified by the advantages accorded to faculty and institutions from a strong and pervasive campus UR culture. An institutional commitment to UR can enrich the curriculum, lead to more creative and dynamic learning environments, generate opportunities for meaningful cross-campus discussions on curricula and pedagogy, foster research collaborations among faculty and departments, and enhance interdisciplinary activities. A successful and unifying UR program can raise institutional reputation and visibility; enhance the recruitment of talented students, faculty, and staff; and attract external funding and committed donors (National Science Board, 1986; National Science Foundation, 1990).

Despite the wide acceptance of the benefits of UR, developing and sustaining an institutional culture of UR is a complex process (Taraban & Blanton, 2008). Many institutions lack the critical leadership to manage the challenging work of transformational change. Deficiencies in campus infrastructure to support dynamic and productive research programs are also prevalent. Many faculty members could benefit from strategies that enable them to generate new research ideas, create time for research, effectively mentor undergraduates, garner external funding, establish successful collaborations, and maintain their level of expertise. Numerous departments seek innovative models for creative research-supportive curricula and for making research experiences more widely accessible to undergraduates.

Thus, the Council on Undergraduate Research's (CUR) National Science Foundation (NSF)–funded project (Malachowski, Ambos, Karukstis, & Osborn, 2010) was designed to develop and enhance UR at a larger scale: within systems/consortia. Our approach is to leverage the synergy of higher education systems and consortia to disseminate effective practices for institutionalizing a culture of UR, utilizing both the amassed organizational experience of CUR and the shared expertise of institutions within a given consortium or system.

Overview of CUR and the Promotion of Undergraduate Research

CUR is a relatively young (37 years as of 2015) higher education nonprofit association. CUR came into existence largely to assert the value of research conducted at predominantly undergraduate, four-year institutions and to provide practical help to individual faculty members seeking to develop UR programs (Doyle, 1987). From its inception in 1978 as an association of 10 chemistry faculty members at predominantly undergraduate institutions in the United States, to its current reality as a vibrant organization of over 10,000 individual and 700 institutional members representing all disciplines and over 900 colleges and universities of all types, CUR has emerged as the primary voice for the global UR movement. The organization has developed an increasingly broad portfolio of programs, services, and advocacy efforts in support of many aspects of the UR enterprise. CUR's work with systems/consortia emphasizes broad-scale, long-term transformational change linked across multiple institutions. The organization's rapid growth, stakeholder diversification, and emergence as the international standard bearer for the UR movement also reflect that transformational change.

Four elements of CUR's recent organizational evolution have both strongly shaped the UR programs described in this theme volume and been shaped by the lessons learned from working with the six systems/consortia. First, CUR's rapid growth and diversification into non-STEM disciplines position CUR as a unique "marketplace" for faculty and administrators from all disciplines and vastly different academic cultures to explore UR as a unifying theory for faculty research and teaching, including recognition/reward structures such as retention, tenure, and promotion. Second, CUR's 2010 merger with the National Conference on Undergraduate Research (NCUR) to form one unified organization has led to an expanded emphasis on student programs, complementing CUR's historic focus on the professional development needs of faculty and institutions. Third, the collaborative writing process, subsequent publication, and widespread dissemination of the seminal document *Characteristics of Excellence in Undergraduate Research* (Hensel, 2012) proved to be a galvanizing focus for the organization, providing high-quality standards for UR programs for the first time. Fourth, CUR's formal adoption of three primary strategic pillars in 2012—broadening participation in UR, embedding UR in the curriculum, and assessing the impacts of UR—signified the organization's readiness to thoroughly connect UR with other domains of higher education policy and thought leadership, particularly the imperative for undergraduate student retention, graduation, and subsequent career success.

History, Scope, and Goals of CUR's "Institutionalizing Undergraduate Research" Workshop Program

One of the main types of professional development meetings that CUR offers is the multiday workshop. The longest running of these is the "Institutionalizing Undergraduate Research" (IUR) workshop through which we have worked with over 450 institutions and over 1,800 faculty members and administrators, representing all types of institutions and disciplines. There have been three distinct phases of this project, and we will describe them next to show the evolution of our engagement with the campuses.

1996–2006: Building Capacity.   Since its inception in 1996, each IUR workshop has been team-based, attracting 8–15 institutional teams nationally, with each participating institution sending a four- to six-person team. At the heart of the workshop is an expectation that each team generate a series of goals to integrate higher levels of UR that would then be adapted and expanded when the team returned to campus.

From 1996 to 2006, the program served over 300 institutions of all types. Several institutions were repeat attendees, developmentally building on their growth and successes at subsequent workshops; one institution attended four times.

2006–2010: Regional Workshops.   One limitation of the annual IUR workshop was that it typically required teams to travel across the country, and these costs were prohibitive for many institutions to send a team. Moreover, the national distribution of participants limited follow-up interactions among attendees.

To address these concerns, with the support of an NSF–Course, Curriculum, and Laboratory Improvement (CCLI) Phase 2 award (Hensel, Karukstis, Osborn, Malachowski, & Singer, 2006), CUR offered a series of eight regional workshops covering the major geographical regions of the United States from 2006 to 2010. The workshops were designed for institutions that did not have a tradition or culture of campus-wide engagement in UR. Each workshop served eight institutions with each institutional team comprising three faculty members and one administrator. Overall, the project engaged 64 institutions and over 256 participants in the initial round of workshops. These workshops included discussion of issues such as implementation/expansion of a research culture, strategies and models for institutionalization, challenges of fostering institutional change, and assessment. Teams worked closely with a trained facilitator to generate an action plan that strategically guided their activities to institutionalize UR across their campuses.

The workshop outcomes were enhanced by a robust series of follow-up activities, including site visits to each of the 64 campuses approximately one year after the initial workshop. At each follow-up visit, a consultant met with 50–100 faculty members and key administrators on each campus, delivered a presentation, facilitated an on-campus retreat, assessed how the plan initially conceived during the workshop had evolved, and provided guidance on next steps for the institution's plan.

Through an extensive external evaluation, about 90% of the attendees stated that they were modifying their UR goals based on what they learned at the workshop and taking action to institutionalize UR on their campuses. These results indicated a strong disposition for institutions to change fundamental campus goals, and they illustrated the broad impact of the workshops and follow-up visits. The project's broadest impact was ensuring the sustainable implementation of UR at the participating institutions and building regional UR communities.

2010–2014: Scaling-Up—System/Consortium Workshops. Although CUR had worked with many institutions since 1996 and had built capacity around the country, there was still a great deal of unmet need as many institutions were articulating their desire to increase adoption of high-impact pedagogies and their overall research efforts. Consequently, in 2010, with the support of an NSF-CCLI Phase 3 award (Malachowski et al., 2010), we comprehensively extended the successful model of working solely with individual institutions to work with larger organizational units that had similar or closely related missions: state systems and public and private consortia.

This workshop program was fundamentally designed to improve the quality of undergraduate education at each of the constituent campuses and within the larger systems/consortia by leveraging the synergy, influence, and power of the systems and consortia.

Twenty-four systems/consortia applied to participate, from which six were selected: the Council on Public Liberal Arts Colleges (COPLAC), the University of Wisconsin State System (UW), the California State University System (CSU), the City University of New York System (CUNY), the Great Lakes Colleges Association (GLCA), and the Pennsylvania State System of Higher Education (PASSHE). Overall, we worked directly with six systems/consortia, 80 institutions, and over 300 faculty members and administrators.

The workshop curricula were tailored to meet the needs of each system/consortium, and the curricula covered such topics as understanding and changing institutional culture, faculty hiring, tenure/promotion and workload issues, curriculum case studies, assessment, funding, supporting nontraditional students, connecting UR to service learning, community-based learning and international education, and promoting UR in all disciplines.

One key difference between this system/consortium workshop project and the earlier regional workshop project was the design and implementation of follow-up activities. Here, we brought together all of the system/consortium participants for a second workshop approximately one year after the initial one. The follow-up workshops were designed to provide support during the critical, one-year-out point in the implementation of action plans; our past experience had taught us that many teams need to be reinvigorated at this juncture. The follow-up workshops were designed to be interactive and discussion based, with the institutional teams helping each other wrestle with their own challenges and sharing lessons learned from their own experiences and best practices developed within each system/consortium.

The project evaluation identified common challenges for system/consortium-level administrators, including obtaining accurate information about the status of UR on their multiple campuses, configuring system assistance to match widely varying campus needs, promoting a reasonably consistent vision for UR across numerous and diverse campuses, and maintaining a shared vision when personnel change at the campus and system/consortium levels. Furthermore, the summative phase of the project helped to develop a better understanding of the processes and the most effective drivers of organizational and culture change.

Workshop Design.   Key to the workshop design was a three-day format that involved team participation, including three faculty members and at least one senior-level administrator from each campus, and system/consortium leaders. The workshop schedule included a strategic balance of presentations, breakout discussions, and networking. Attention was focused both on serving the needs of each campus and, most importantly, on fostering connections among the system/consortium and their member institutions.

Workshop Goals and Outcomes.   Each workshop was designed to achieve four interconnected goals: (a) provide teams with information on the status and landscape of UR at the national level; (b) help each system/consortium in building and enhancing a culture that supports UR, both at the individual institution level and the system/consortium level; (c) assist the system/consortium and the constituent campuses in articulating goals for institutionalizing UR, as well as developing strategies to achieve these goals on each campus; and (d) help identify common challenges and opportunities among the campuses, and help develop an integrated approach, supported by the central office, that would aid in expanding UR capacity throughout the system/consortium.

Each team worked closely with a trained facilitator who guided the team's efforts and ensured that challenging, but realistic, goals were set. The facilitators played a crucial role in the success of the workshops, and we carefully selected facilitators for their range of experiences, understanding of the national issues, and, most importantly, their ability to both facilitate the work of the teams and help them dream big while generating realistic goals. At the completion of each workshop, every institutional team left with a customized and action-oriented plan that would strategically guide their implementation activities to institutionalize UR on their own campus. The system/consortium office also developed a coordinated plan to embed and sustain UR as a central pedagogical and scholarly endeavor within the entire system/consortium. The resulting action plans included a mission statement and short-, medium-, and long-term goals (each with planned strategies, timelines, pertinent stakeholders, and assessment plans to achieve those goals and measure progress toward them) that were brought back to their campuses for implementation.

Strategies Used: An Overview of the Volume

Embedding UR across an individual campus requires considerable cooperation and an ability to work through many hurdles among the many campus units. Performing the same undertaking across an entire system or consortium magnifies the challenges enormously and requires a much higher level of planning and execution. This challenge is at the heart of our work on this project, and our understanding of how systems and consortia function is a key component of our interactions with them.

In the chapters that follow, each of the six systems/consortia that participated in the project provides a synopsis of their work to institutionalize UR, with each narrative focusing on a different pressing higher education topic. Outcomes from the institutional teams, their impacts at the system/consortium level, and different strategies used to institutionalize UR are described. Two additional chapters focus on the broader perspective of organizational/cultural change at the system/consortium level.

Chapter 2: The 30,000-Foot View From the National Association of System Heads and the Center for Inquiry in the Liberal Arts. This chapter describes issues that revolve around how particular cultures of each system/consortium inform organizational change at both the macro and micro level. Profiles of each system/consortium are provided and connections to their modes of action and strategies pursued are considered.

Issues of "systemness" are probed, and questions such as how particular components of systems/consortia facilitate the measurement and scaling-up of UR are discussed. This chapter breaks new ground in addressing the question of whether there are effective system/consortium strategies that can be used to maximize outputs for any activity, including UR.

Chapter 3: California State University System. Here the focus shifts to a discussion of the impact of UR on students from underrepresented groups and how it connects to the CSU's push for student success. There is a natural connection between UR and CSU's Graduation Initiative, as UR has been shown to have substantial impacts on underrepresented students. Finding ways to engage all students on a given campus is critical to student success. These initiatives are challenging because many students juggle family needs and/or jobs that make it difficult to engage in UR.

This chapter lays out many of the challenges that any system/institution/department faces in trying to embed UR within its programs, including the crucial need to focus on sustainability. Consideration is given to issues such as funding for students and faculty, community engagement, an undergraduate journal, celebration days, links to community colleges, and developing research-rich curricula. The CSU system has worked hard to build connections across their diverse campuses through the use of affinity groups and efforts of the central office. Paramount in the CSU approach is its impact on retention and graduation success. Data collection and utilization are critically important in the system, so a discussion of how the CSU uses assessment dashboards is included.

Chapter 4: University of Wisconsin System. In this chapter, leaders from the UW system describe their efforts to connect UR to economic development, workforce development, and innovation. This is an important element of campus research endeavors in Wisconsin, and UR is shown to connect strongly with these statewide initiatives. The development of partnerships within and outside the campuses is a large component of these efforts, with technology transfer among all the parties in the state being critically important. Numerous examples and case studies of successful collaborations between· campuses and industrial partners are described along with their direct connections to undergraduates. UR serves the state well, and many initiatives have been undertaken to strengthen student outcomes while connecting undergraduates with innovation and economic development efforts.

Chapter 5: Council of Public Liberal Arts Colleges. UR is an activity that clearly has a focus on students and student learning. However, it also impacts faculty in many ways, including issues that revolve around faculty workload and tenure/promotion, and these are described in this chapter. Leaders from COPLAC discuss the many facets of faculty professional pursuits and consider maximizing faculty support while enhancing student outcomes.

Given the diversity of faculty needs, success for these endeavors is connected to faculty buy-in of the teacher–scholar model. Strengthening connections among all the participants can challenge campuses, so COPLAC describes how they used surveys to collect valuable data about the prevalence and scope of UR activities across the consortium, from both the faculty and student perspectives, and created an innovative distance-mentoring program.

Chapter 6: Pennsylvania State System of Higher Education. High-impact practices, including UR, are powerful ways to impact student outcomes. Leaders from PASSHE describe connections among high-impact practices and focus on the centrality of UR in these efforts. This chapter describes the drivers that have helped move UR front and center at many PASSHE campuses. This conversation focuses on how PASSHE has dealt with state funding declines and differential demographics across the system, and how the system office can support and drive initiatives that promote UR as a system-wide solution.

Despite serious financial stress, enrollment declines, and retrenchment of tenured faculty members at some institutions, UR has been used as a vehicle to meet or exceed system-wide student graduation and equity targets. As a result, UR has been shown to be a driver for enrollment management efforts related to student retention, and the conversation is now centered on UR as an investment rather than as an expense. Connections to PASSHE's performance enhancement model are used to illustrate the power of system-incentivized UR to foster deep levels of student learning across the system.

Chapter 7: City University of New York System. UR usually requires different types of resources for success. Here, leaders from CUNY discuss the landscape for securing funding to support and enhance high-quality UR activities. Funding has become a particularly challenging aspect for all forms of CUNY research, including UR. In many cases, faculty spend enormous amounts of time trying to both identify opportunities and procure funding, so it's important to connect conversations about UR outcomes and impacts to the issues that help get projects off the ground.

This chapter uses case studies from three CUNY campuses to link UR to internal and external sources of funding. Descriptions of community college funding, and how this helps shape their UR focus and programs, curriculum-based projects, and the apprentice model of UR are also presented.

Chapter 8: Great Lakes Colleges Association. One-on-one mentored UR experiences provide some of the most powerful experiences in which undergraduates can be involved. However, one of the challenges for these undertakings is how to engage all students when faculty time and resources are limited. Integrating research into curricula effectively addresses these concerns and provides all students with more equitable access to UR benefits. Here, GLCA leaders discuss connecting UR to the curriculum, particularly as a foundation for long-standing senior capstone courses with UR being a primary component. Three case studies from GLCA institutions are used to highlight the time and effort devoted to curriculum development within the consortium and the role UR plays within a course, program, and general education. Disciplinarily appropriate, inquiry-driven assignments scaffolded throughout the curriculum achieve many student outcomes, and this approach is articulated. Curricular coherence is one of the goals of the GLCA programs, and this issue is also addressed.

Chapter 9: Fostering Change at the System/Consortium Level. The greatest challenge faced by every team that has attended our workshops is the expectation that they will lead a transformative change process once they return to campus. At the workshops, we devote extensive training and coaching to the elements of institutional change and the factors that determine levels of change, but it is still daunting for participants to lead and sustain those efforts.

In this concluding chapter, we discuss the lessons learned from our interactions with the six systems/consortia and describe the key challenges to the high-level change that we collectively have been working toward and the importance of leadership and stability at the system/consortium offices and on the campuses. However, it is clear that the one characteristic that matters most is changing the institutional culture, particularly in the importance of connecting faculty research, scholarship, and creative activity to the undergraduate experience. We conclude the volume with a discussion of conditions needed to effect transformative change in UR, both at the individual campus level and for a system/consortium as a whole.

References

Brew, A. (2010). Imperatives and challenges in integrating teaching and research. *Higher Education Research & Development*, 29(2), 139–150.

Doyle, M. P. (1987). Editorial comments: The new NSF-REU program is not the return of the URP program. *CUR Newsletter*, 7(2), 3–4.

Hathaway, R. S., Nagda, B., & Gregerman, S. (2002). The relationship of undergraduate research participation to graduate and professional education pursuit: An empirical study. *Journal of College Student Development*, 43(5), 614–631.

Hensel, N. (2012). *Characteristics of excellence in undergraduate research*. Washington, DC: Council on Undergraduate Research.

Hensel, N., Karukstis, K., Osborn, J., Malachowski, M., & Singer, J. (2006). *A workshop initiative by the Council on Undergraduate Research to establish, enhance, and institutionalize undergraduate research* (NSF-DUE #0618721).

Hu, S., Scheuch, K., Schwartz, R., Gayles, J. G., & Li, S. (2008). *Reinventing undergraduate education: Engaging college students in research and creative activities* [ASHE Higher Education Report, 33(4)]. Hoboken, NJ: Wiley.

Hunter, A. B., Laursen, S. L., & Seymour, E. (2006). Becoming a scientist. *Science Education*, 91, 36–74.

Kardash, C. A. (2000). Evaluation of an undergraduate research experience: Perceptions of undergraduate interns and their faculty mentors. *Journal of Educational Psychology*, 92, 191–201.

Kuh, G. (2008). *High-impact educational practices: What they are, who has access to them, and why they matter*. Washington, DC: AAC&U.

Kuh, G. D., Kinzie, J., Schuh, J. H., Whitt, E. J., & Associates. (2010). *Student success in college: Creating conditions that matter*. San Francisco, CA: Wiley.

Laursen, S., Hunter, A.-B., Seymour, E., Thiry, H., & Melton, G. (2010). *Undergraduate research in the sciences: Engaging students in real science*. San Francisco, CA: Jossey-Bass.

Laursen, S., Seymour, E., & Hunter, A.-B. (2012). Learning, teaching and scholarship: Fundamental tensions of undergraduate research. *Change: The Magazine of Higher Learning*, 44(2), 30–37.

Lopatto, D. (2009). *Science in solution: The impact of undergraduate research on student learning*. Tucson, AZ: The Research Corporation for Science Advancement.

Malachowski, M., Ambos, E., Karukstis, K., & Osborn, J. (2010). *Collaborative research: Transformational learning through undergraduate research: Comprehensive support for faculty, institutions, state systems and consortia* (NSF-DUE #0920275, #0920286).

National Science Board. (1986). *Undergraduate science, mathematics and engineering education*. Washington, DC: Author.

National Science Foundation. (1990). *NSF's research experiences for undergraduates (REU) program: An assessment of the first three years*. Washington, DC: Author.

Osborn, J. M., & Karukstis, K. K. (2009). The benefits of undergraduate research, scholarship, and creative activity. In M. Boyd & J. Wesemann (Eds.), *Broadening participation in undergraduate research: Fostering excellence and enhancing the impact* (pp. 41–53). Washington, DC: Council on Undergraduate Research.

Seymour, E., Hunter, A.-B., Laursen, S. L., & DeAntoni, T. (2004). Establishing the benefits of research experiences for undergraduates: First findings from a three-year study. *Science Education*, 88, 493–534.

Taraban, R., & Blanton, R. L. (Eds.). (2008). *Creating effective undergraduate research programs in science: The transformation from student to scientist.* New York, NY: Teachers College Press.

MITCHELL MALACHOWSKI *is a professor of chemistry at the University of San Diego and a coordinator of CUR's Institutionalizing Undergraduate Research Program.*

JEFFREY M. OSBORN *is the dean of the School of Science and professor of biology at The College of New Jersey, and a coordinator of CUR's Institutionalizing Undergraduate Research Program.*

KERRY K. KARUKSTIS *is the Ray and Mary Ingwersen Professor and chair of chemistry at Harvey Mudd College, and a coordinator of CUR's Institutionalizing Undergraduate Research Program.*

ELIZABETH L. AMBOS *is the executive officer of the Council on Undergraduate Research.*

NEW DIRECTIONS FOR HIGHER EDUCATION • DOI: 10.1002/he

2

This chapter examines the role of systems and consortia in scaling and implementing undergraduate research through a study of the efforts of six systems and consortia working together with the Council on Undergraduate Research.

The System Effect: Scaling High-Impact Practices Across Campuses

Jonathan S. Gagliardi, Rebecca R. Martin, Kathleen Wise, Charles Blaich

Introduction

Amid an environment fraught with change, our U.S. system of higher education is shifting. These changes have led to growing interest and research on systems and consortia in higher education (e.g., Zimpher, 2013). Much of that work has been centered on the change efforts of systems to meet increasingly complex demands in a dizzying environment (e.g., Lane & Johnstone, 2013; McGuinness, 1996). Systems, like the campuses they serve, are composed of a collection of people, processes, structures, cultures, and norms that are constantly shifting (e.g., Martinez & Smith, 2013). In the past, systems have served as regulators, allocators, and coordinators of the campuses contained within them (e.g., Lane & Johnstone, 2013). Today, systems are seen as drivers of social mobility and economic growth. For systems and campuses to continue to honor their promise of access and opportunity, they must react to changes that include: (a) growing demand for postsecondary access and success, (b) heightened accountability among various actors, (c) trends of divestment or stagnant public funding, and (d) technological and analytical advancements that have grown expectations (e.g., Etzkowitz & Leydesdorff, 2000; Gagliardi & Wellman, 2014; Perna & Finney, 2014). As such, a deeper knowledge of how systems are changing to meet those needs has grown in importance, particularly surrounding student access and success.

Emerging literature and media suggest that, if harnessed effectively, systems can wield greater influence than the individual institutions that comprise them, particularly by creating economies of scale and scope in high-impact practices (Kuh, 2008). Recognizing that there is a gap in the research

New Directions for Higher Education, no. 169, Spring 2015 © 2015 Wiley Periodicals, Inc.
Published online in Wiley Online Library (wileyonlinelibrary.com) • DOI: 10.1002/he.20119

on the ability of systems and consortia to effectively scale such practices leads to a series of questions: How do particular components of systems and consortia facilitate the measurement and scaling of high-impact practices, such as undergraduate research? Are there effective system and consortium strategies that can be used to magnify the impact of such efforts? How can systems and consortia facilitate collaboration among campuses surrounding prioritizing undergraduate research across their member campuses?

This chapter examines the role of systems and consortia in scaling and implementing undergraduate research (UR) through a study of the efforts of six systems and consortia to do so. Insight is provided into these questions by distilling efforts described within strategic frameworks and initiatives launched during a series of workshops convened by the Council on Undergraduate Research (CUR) to help scale and prioritize UR (Malachowski, Ambos, Karukstis, & Osborn, 2010).

An Overview of the Development of Higher Education Systems

Today, higher education systems are in the center of what Martinez and Smith (2013) refer to as "the higher education ecosystem" (p. 169). There are multiple system-level actors, which include the system head and the system-level staff. Typically, systems report to a governing board that is charged with setting policy and procedures (e.g., McGuinness, 2013). System offices typically interact with myriad stakeholders, including campuses, governing boards, coordinating boards, and the legislature. Those interactions, particularly between the system and campuses, and system and legislature, are key to the effectiveness of a system (Lane & Johnstone, 2013). The ability of a system to carefully balance campus autonomy with system-level collaboration and coordination on a key set of initiatives often dictates whether or not the system is perceived as a resource or as a burden (Lane & Johnstone, 2013; Zimpher, 2013).

Consortia of colleges and universities lack the statutory authority found in public university systems, but they share many of the goals around shared resources, scaling best practices, and meeting the changing needs of society. Such consortia are drawn together based on shared mission, similar campus configuration, or geographic proximity. Given CUR's long-standing relationships with many institutions outside of public university systems, consortia form an important approach to collective work with multiple campuses.

Ongoing Environmental and Systemic Changes

In higher education, there is growing interest in leveraging organizations to create economies of scale and scope by using the centralized role of postsecondary systems (Lane & Johnstone, 2013). This, according to Lane and Johnstone (2013), is because higher education systems serve as "boundary spanners" that connect campuses, legislatures, the private sector, and civic society (Scott & Davis, 2007). While connected to all, systems lack full affiliation with any, which affords them the opportunity to advocate and govern competing interests among these diverse stakeholders. Advantages to organizing as a system or consortium include greater efficiencies, coordination and quality, academic integrity, differentiation, insulation from competition, and a sharp and collective focus on the needs of students and communities.

The Implications of a Shifting Landscape for Systems

For decades, systems proved effective vehicles for social mobility and economic growth. However, within an environment that is ever-changing, systems are being asked to redouble their efforts surrounding postsecondary access and success, equity gaps, and external accountability despite ongoing trends of shrinking or stagnant public funding in higher education (e.g., Lane & Johnstone, 2013; Perna & Finney, 2014). Inadequate improvements in student outcomes and a turbulent environment have led systems and consortia to adapt in ways that include: (a) strengthening the vitality of the campuses that comprise them, (b) coordinating the work of campuses across shared goals and strategies, and (c) leveraging the collective capacity of campuses toward improved student outcomes. These efforts to better position systems and consortia to create economies of scale and scope may result in increasing efficiencies that allow for resources to be reallocated toward student success (Clark, 1988; Junius, 1997). Specifically, systems and consortia and campuses are targeting high-impact practices, such as scaling UR (Kuh, 2008).

CUR has worked to advance UR at the campus level through an array of efforts designed to broaden participation, identify characteristics of excellence, and develop a research-supportive curriculum, among others (e.g., Boyd & Wesemann, 2009; Cooke & Thorne, 2011; Hensel, 2012; Karukstis & Elgren, 2007). The centralized position of the system to connect and scale UR is a potential mechanism for expanding upon the campus approach to advance UR, given the ubiquity of student success imperatives across campuses.

UR in System/Consortial Settings

In recognition of the potential benefits of involving systems and consortia in scaling UR, CUR designed a series of activities and workshops intended to help systems and consortia sustain efforts to do so (Malachowski et al., 2010). CUR leadership aimed to supplement the impact of its workshops by

New Directions for Higher Education • DOI: 10.1002/he

Figure 2.1. Original Support Structure of CUR Workshops

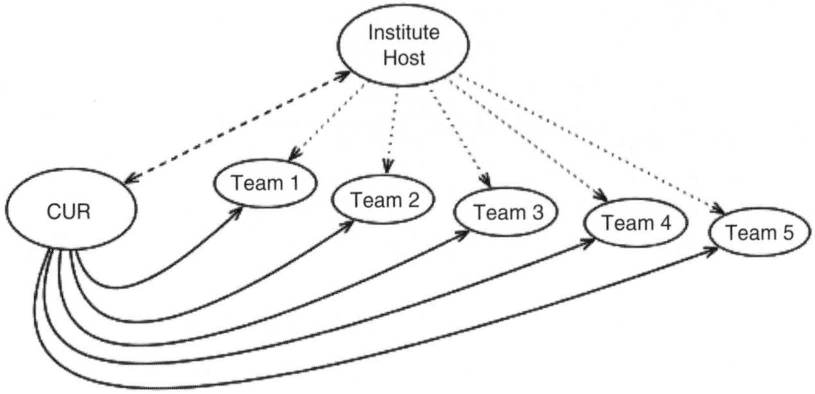

shifting from having CUR and CUR facilitators serve as the sole persistent support for participating institutions following a workshop (Figure 2.1) to having both CUR and the system/consortium offices provide a persistent and more robust connection with institutions (Figure 2.2).

The success of this approach depends on whether system offices have the capacity to foster communication and collaboration, to monitor progress, and to offer direct support to assist in overcoming challenges as they emerge for member campuses. A deeper assumption is that the "challenging work of transformational change throughout the system/consortia" on UR would be one of the top priorities of the system/consortium offices.

Figure 2.2. Support Structure With System/Consortium Incorporated

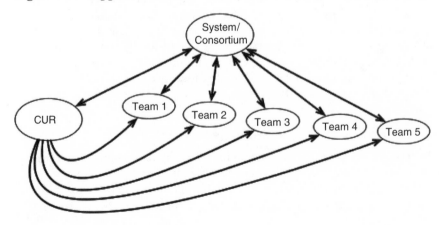

Study of the Outcomes of CUR Professional Development for Systems/Consortia

The purpose of our study is to explore the impact of a system-based approach to UR. We sought to do this by reviewing the findings on the factors that influence the capacity of systems and consortia to develop and extend UR programs in the member systems and consortia and to inform future system efforts at scaling and implementing high-impact UR programs. A study of system and consortia efforts to implement UR efforts was undertaken with six participating systems and consortia. From this analysis, prevailing themes and cross-cutting issues were identified to inform future efforts to scale UR through a system.

System Profiles.   The six systems and consortia that participated in this study included:

- California State University System (CSU)
- City University of New York System (CUNY)
- Pennsylvania State System of Higher Education (PASSHE)
- University of Wisconsin System (UW)
- Council of Public Liberal Arts Colleges (COPLAC)
- Great Lakes Colleges Association (GLCA)

These systems and consortia have considerable variation in the number of institutions, undergraduate enrollment, staff size, and geographical distribution of member institutions (Table 2.1).

Governance Implications for UR Change?   The public systems that were convened as part of this project have a much deeper and hierarchical structure that is visibly more bureaucratic when compared to participating consortia. Participating consortia may have more nimble structures, but there are also additional barriers to scaling. For example, there were instances where consortium member institutions belong to other public

Table 2.1. System and Consortia Characteristics

	Number of Four-Year Institutions	Approximate System/ Consortia Staff Size	Number of States	Approximate FTE Undergraduates[a]
COPLAC	27	4	25[b]	94,000
CSU	23	520	1	310,000
PASSHE	14	180	1	97,000
CUNY	11	1,240	1	109,000
GLCA	10	8	4	23,000
UW	13	200	1	130,000

[a]At four-year institutions.
[b]COPLAC also includes one institution in Canada.

university systems, creating a duplicative hierarchical structure that may create competing interests and more difficult coordination. Yet, there were still signs that systems and consortia sought to discover ways to circumvent structures and policies that obstruct the scaling of UR, particularly around academic policies that have traditionally been controlled by campuses, many of which relate to faculty.

While public university system and consortium offices vary considerably in size, they share important characteristics that are important to understand in the context of this work. Still, limitations were apparent in ability of some system leaders to be actively involved in scaling UR on their campuses (National Association of System Heads [NASH] & National Center for Higher Education Management Systems [NCHEMS], 2012).

Although the size, complexity, and number of constituencies to whom they are accountable are much greater for the four public systems than the two consortia, we found little difference in the way that the system and consortium officers spoke about the challenges, constraints, and strategies for working with member campuses on scaling UR. Regardless of system or consortium structure, the central office was careful in their expense of political capital as it pertained to generating support for scaling UR. That six diverse systems and consortia chose to engage with willing campuses rather than leverage manifest forms of authority or influence suggests that such an approach is perhaps a more preferable and more effective method of engaging and harnessing the collective capacity of campuses within and across systems.

The Power to Convene.   Systems and consortia have approached the scaling of UR by leveraging the power of convening and incentivizing. Consequences of a diplomatic approach may include tempered and decentralized implementation and progress. Moreover, it does not take full advantage of the governance authorities that the participating systems possess but are sometimes reluctant to use. Navigating high turnover among senior leaders, varying levels of declining enrollment revenues, and mounting facilities and infrastructure costs are all challenges that are more complex the less centralized scaling efforts are. To that end, the systems and consortia's ability to convene is a critical tool that can mitigate the risks inherent in multicampus initiatives. As such, the power of the convening cannot be underscored enough.

As one system officer put it, "Each institution will do things in different ways. They may not do the same things and even if they do, it won't look the same way on each campus." The more that system and consortium officers know the cultural, historical, and political landscapes of member campuses, the more likely they will be able to support campus teams that are working to initiate or expand their UR programs.

A comprehensive understanding of their constituencies allowed the system or consortium office to develop and implement a coordinated plan for further institutionalizing UR.

New Directions for Higher Education • DOI: 10.1002/he

Declining or Stagnant Resources and Economic Growth. All member institutions were dealing with major budget reductions. Of course, these reductions will have an immediate impact on the institutional plans developed at the workshops. This uncertainty has given rise to tensions that compromise collaboration and promote competition, within and across campuses, acting as counterweights to the benefits of a system and consortium approach. People frame the value of workshops with system and consortium member institutions as an opportunity to learn how to improve their own programs, not to help other programs at other institutions get better. Unfortunately, a great deal of evidence suggests that we are in a sustained period of diminished resources (State Higher Education Executive Officers [SHEEO], 2013).

Cross-Cutting Themes for System/Consortial Change in UR

These recent efforts to scale UR across systems and consortia offer insights to researchers, system and consortium leaders and staff, and campus leaders and staff. A series of cross-cutting themes arose from an analysis of system and consortia efforts to scale UR with the help of CUR.

Cross-cutting theme 1: Systems and consortia are well positioned to initiate multicampus projects. Nearly all of the participating systems and consortia had the capacity to write grant proposals, whether through a dedicated office or staff. However, although grant writing is a focused, deadline-driven, and typically short-term activity, it is fundamentally different from the longer term work necessary to change campus cultures and structures to spread a high-impact practice like UR. Sustaining the enthusiasm and productive conversations from the workshops proved very challenging. In most cases, system and consortium offices were not set up to drive such change initiatives on their campuses.

Cross-cutting theme 2: Due to their centralized position systems/consortia are adept at communicating collective impact to stakeholders, particularly external ones. Given that systems and consortia are natural boundary spanners between legislators, the private sector, civic society, and the campuses they serve, they are uniquely positioned to highlight the value of scaling efforts, including efforts to institutionalize UR. The notion that systems/consortia and campuses are chiefly responsible for the education of students and stewards of economic and community development is firmly embedded within the legislation that created them and the mission and values of each respective organization. As such, one particularly important role of systems and consortia is to communicate the importance of scaling the high-impact practice of UR to stakeholders who have indirect interest in such activities.

Cross-cutting theme 3: To move forward, campuses must be engaged and mutually invested in successful collaboration surrounding UR. Systems and consortia that were involved in the CUR workshops were grateful for the opportunity to engage their member campuses around a specific area of focus. Many attendees commented on the newfound energy that resulted from the intensive collaboration that occurred during both the application process and the workshops. Intense focus on strategies of mutual interest strengthened relationships, at least temporarily. Yet, that renewed energy and willingness to collaborate between systems/consortia and the campuses that composed them were difficult to sustain. This can be partially attributed to cultural and functional differences between systems and consortia and their individual campuses. Systems and consortia function in ways that promote greater collaboration and cumulative success among their campuses and have served such a role since their inception. Campuses, on the other hand, are accustomed to functioning autonomously.

Cross-cutting theme 4: "No mandates: working with coalitions of the willing." This heading is a quote from one of the system officers with whom we spoke, and it reflects a sentiment we heard at every system and consortium—the desire of system and consortium leaders to form coalitions of the willing rather than to impose, mandate, or require participation of member institutions in projects. System and consortium initiatives that aim to engage a coalition of willing campuses can help to sustain momentum and bridge cultural and competitive divides. In essence, when it comes to projects like the CUR project, system and consortium officers worked with member institutions in much the same way that academic leaders work with academic faculty and departments—they try to build a "critical mass" of volunteers to build interest in increasingly broader circles.

Cross-cutting theme 5: System and consortium offices have limited knowledge of what is happening on member campuses. More timely and high-quality data, as well as standards across campuses, are needed to promote the scaling of UR. Systems and consortia can only work to create more effective campus partnerships and economies of scale when they are aware of ongoing initiatives. Moreover, what data that do exist are unstandardized, making it difficult to compare institutional efforts at promoting and scaling UR in addition to measuring progress. Making better information available to system leadership, such as the ongoing development of a data system at the CSU that includes measures related to UR, is a critical next step in the effective scaling of UR efforts.

Models for System/Consortium Support of Institutionalizing UR

Several effective approaches to this work emerged from this project.

- The PASSHE system comes closest to taking system-level actions that could embed UR as a central pedagogical and scholarly endeavor across the system. All member institutions in the PASSHE system participated in both workshops, and the participants on the institutional teams were very consistent. The vice-chancellor of the system was articulate in connecting the pedagogy of UR to the system's most important strategic initiatives, and the system office developed a communication strategy that kept the project in front of member institutions' presidents, chief academic officers, and the Board of Trustees. The expansion of UR was linked to the national and statewide initiatives in which PASSHE was participating and to the long-term educational impact and financial health of the system. UR was seen as a means of improving retention, reducing the achievement gap for less prepared students, and marketing PASSHE institutions to prospective students. The system sought to reward campuses and faculty that had higher levels of UR with more funding.

• In the University of Wisconsin System, member institutions were willing to take a leadership role, in coordination with the system office, and work with leaders at other system institutions to advance UR at their institutions. These campus leaders held ongoing meetings between advocates for UR from the different system institutions. Moreover, the system also presented the project to the Board of Trustees, which was very powerful. This distributed leadership model for a collective effort could strengthen a system-wide approach.

• The California State University System has a model for a systemic approach to campus-based high-impact practices in their Center for Community Engagement, which funds a dedicated service learning position on each campus and leads ongoing efforts to support this work. While they have yet to establish this level of system-wide investment in UR, they are providing support through centralized activities such as a long-standing system-wide student research competition and the development of new metrics for tracking UR and student success.

Given the array of local contexts among the institutions in systems and consortia, we believe system and consortial leaders must publicly articulate the importance of UR and how it connects with other system-level initiatives, engage a sufficient number of member institutions to form a potential community of practice, promote UR to member campus leaders, keep the project in front of member campus provosts and deans, create mechanisms to help people on campuses who are implementing plans stay connected, and disseminate information about success stories to teams on member campuses.

Conclusions and Implications

The following implications may be drawn from the key themes that emerged from CUR's engagement with systems and consortia. First, for systems and consortia to successfully scale UR, campuses must be equally invested in the success of such efforts. Systems and consortia are uniquely positioned to convene similarly minded campuses surrounding UR. This power cannot be underestimated, as it allows systems and consortia to clearly define the scaling strategy, which allows for campuses to fit ongoing activities within an agreed upon approach to scaling UR.

Second, as many states reduce public funding and attach more performance incentives to the funding they do provide, the need to demonstrate progress and sustainability has implications for future support. The lack of standard measures and an inability to demonstrate impact at the individual campus, let alone across a system or consortium, must be resolved. Third, the ability of system and consortium offices to initiate and coordinate initiatives as well as to communicate those effectively to external audiences is a strength that could apply to many student-success-related initiatives underway in the academy. Additionally, systems and consortia offer the benefits of efficiency, scale, and scope that can free institutions to focus on the tailored implementation needed for successful change. Further, system and consortium offices offer strong agency and advocacy on behalf of campuses as they make efforts to change strategically.

The efforts of CUR to work with systems and consortia have uncovered the strengths and limitations of system- and consortium-led initiatives and identified effective approaches between systems/consortia and member campuses to broaden the levels of UR. Questions for future consideration include the following:

- What are the optimal staffing models and decision-making structures at the system and consortia levels that would best complement the academic and student affairs personnel on individual campuses?
- How can systems and consortia create a platform for change that attains scale and scope and that allows individual campuses the ability to customize such efforts to account for their uniqueness?
- Given the vast differences in capacity to measure and monitor the progress of efforts to scale UR among campuses, can the system aid in the collection of data and creation of mutually agreed upon metrics outlining trends in UR?
- Can initiatives that exist across the systems and consortia be used to build synergies with member campuses and the academic and student affairs personnel residing within them?

While the findings of this study revealed that there is still much to understand to achieve optimal system- and consortium-wide efforts to improve student outcomes, they also illustrate that there is much to gain from doing so.

References

Boyd, M. K., & Wesemann, J. L. (2009). *Broadening participation in undergraduate research: Fostering excellence and enhancing the impact.* Washington, DC: Council on Undergraduate Research.

Clark, J. A. (1988). Economies of scale and scope at depository financial institutions: A review of literature. *Economic Review, Federal Reserve Bank of Kansas City, 73*(8), 16–33.

Cooke, D., & Thorne, T. (2011). *A practical handbook for supporting community-based research with undergraduate students.* Washington, DC: Council on Undergraduate Research.

Etzkowitz, H., & Leydesdorff, L. (2000). The dynamics of innovation: From National Systems and "Mode 2" to a Triple Helix of university-industry-government relations. *Research Policy, 29*(2), 109–123.

Gagliardi, J. S., & Wellman, J. (2014). *Meeting demands for improvements in public system institutional research: Progress report on the NASH project in IR.* Retrieved from http://www.nashonline.org/sites/default/files/attachments/nash-ir-report.pdf

Hensel, N. (Ed.). (2012). *Characteristics of excellence in undergraduate research.* Washington, DC: Council on Undergraduate Research.

Junius, K. (1997). *Economies of scale: A survey of empirical literature.* Kiel, Germany: Kiel Institute of World Economics.

Karukstis, K. K., & Elgren, T. E. (2007). *Developing and sustaining a research supportive curriculum: A compendium of successful practices.* Washington, DC: Council on Undergraduate Research.

Kuh, G. D. (2008). *High-impact educational practices: What they are, who has access to them, and why they matter.* Washington, DC: Association of American Colleges and Universities.

Lane, J. E., & Johnstone, D. B. (Eds.). (2013). *Higher education systems 3.0: Harnessing systemness, delivering performance.* Albany: State University of New York Press.

Malachowski, M., Ambos, E., Karukstis, K., & Osborn, J. (2010). *Collaborative research: Transformational learning through undergraduate research: Comprehensive support for faculty, institutions, state systems and consortia* (NSF-DUE #0920275, #0920286).

Martinez, M., & Smith, B. (2013). Systems, ecosystems, and change in state-level public higher education. In J. E. Lane & D. B. Johnstone (Eds.), *Higher education systems 3.0: Exploring the opportunities & challenges of systemness* (pp. 169–192). Albany, NY: SUNY Press.

McGuinness, A. C., Jr. (1996). A model for successful restructuring. In T. J. MacTaggart (Ed.), *Restructuring higher education: What works and what doesn't in reorganizing governing systems* (pp. 203–229). San Francisco, CA: Jossey-Bass.

McGuinness, A. C., Jr. (2013). The history and evolution of higher education systems in the United States. In J. E. Lane & D. B. Johnstone (Eds.), *Higher education systems 3.0: Exploring the opportunities & challenges of systemness* (pp. 45–74). Albany, NY: SUNY Press.

National Association of System Heads (NASH) & National Center for Higher Education Management Systems (NCHEMS). (2012). *A survey of multi-campus system offices.* Washington, DC: National Association of System Heads and National Center for Higher Education Management Systems.

Perna, L. W., & Finney, J. (2014). *The attainment agenda: State policy leadership in higher education.* Baltimore, MD: Johns Hopkins University Press.

Scott, W. R., & Davis, G. F. (2007). *Organizations and organizing: Rational, natural, and open systems perspectives.* Upper Saddle River, NJ: Pearson Prentice Hall.

State Higher Education Executive Officers (SHEEO). (2013). *State higher education finance report, FY 2012.* Retrieved from http://www.sheeo.org/sites/default/files/publications/SHEF%20FY%2012-20130322rev.pdf

Zimpher, N. L. (2013). Systemness: Unpacking the value of higher education. In J. E. Lane & D. B. Johnstone (Eds.), *Higher education systems 3.0: Exploring the opportunities & challenges of systemness* (pp. 27–44). Albany, NY: SUNY Press.

JONATHAN S. GAGLIARDI *currently serves as the deputy director of the National Association of System Heads.*

REBECCA R. MARTIN *is the executive director of the National Association of System Heads.*

KATHLEEN WISE *is the associate director of the Center of Inquiry and the director of the Teagle Assessment Scholar Program.*

CHARLES BLAICH *is the director of the Center of Inquiry and the Higher Education Data Sharing Consortium.*

3

This chapter captures the mission and spirit of the California State University in its efforts to institutionalize undergraduate research and support the success of students traditionally underrepresented in higher education.

Undergraduate Research and Its Impact on Student Success for Underrepresented Students

Ken O'Donnell, Judy Botelho, Jessica Brown, Gerardo M. González, William Head

The California State University System

The California State University (CSU) System is the nation's largest four-year public university system. We educate 437,000 students on our 23 campuses, 87% of whom are undergraduates, with over 76,000 bachelor's degrees conferred annually. The CSU draws students from the top third of the state's high school graduates, placing it between the more selective University of California system and the open-access California Community Colleges. As an access-oriented institution, we are charged with advancing the state's economic growth, civic vitality, and upward mobility.

Many of our students come from groups that are underserved by higher education: economically disadvantaged, first in their families to attend college, and ethnic minorities. In fall 2012, 37% of CSU students were of Hispanic/Latino, African American, or American Indian decent (CSU, 2013; Figure 3.1). We award more than half of all undergraduate degrees granted to students from these groups in California.

The CSU reaffirmed its commitment to enhance student access to active learning, including undergraduate research, in its 2008 management plan, *Access to Excellence* (CSU, 2008). The plan pointed to the capture and replication of best-practice models and applied research infrastructure as important next steps toward this major institutional goal.

NEW DIRECTIONS FOR HIGHER EDUCATION, no. 169, Spring 2015 © 2015 Wiley Periodicals, Inc.
Published online in Wiley Online Library (wileyonlinelibrary.com) • DOI: 10.1002/he.20120

Figure 3.1. Fall 2012 Enrollment by Ethnicity

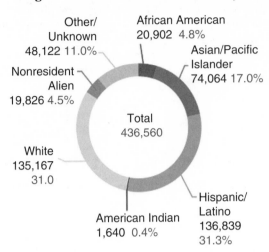

Other/
Unknown
48,122 11.0%

African American
20,902 4.8%

Asian/Pacific
Islander
74,064 17.0%

Nonresident
Alien
19,826 4.5%

Total
436,560

White
135,167
31.0

American Indian
1,640 0.4%

Hispanic/
Latino
136,839
31.3%

Impact of Undergraduate Research on Underrepresented Student Success

Due to changing demographics, evolving workforce needs, and recognition of the democratizing effect of diverse campuses (Gurin, Nagda, & Lopez, 2004), the success of underrepresented minorities is now a state and national priority. Launched in 2009, the CSU's Graduation Initiative is working to halve the gap in underrepresented student degree attainment by 2015. Nationally, there are calls for increased degree attainment by underrepresented students in the science, technology, engineering, and mathematics (STEM) fields (Malcom, Dowd, & Yu, 2010).

The CSU's investment in "high-impact practices," including service learning, peer mentoring, and undergraduate research, is paying off. At California State University Northridge (CSUN), for example, there is a strong correlation between graduation rates and participation in multiple high-impact practices, particularly for Latino students (Figure 3.2). Service learning has benefited from system-wide coordination and infrastructure support through the CSU Center for Community Engagement. We seek to replicate this systematic approach with undergraduate research to serve our diverse students and close the graduation attainment gap.

The benefits of undergraduate research on underrepresented students are well documented. Students who participate in research gain hands-on experience, have more applied learning opportunities (Hunter, Laursen, & Seymour, 2006; Laursen, Seymour, Hunter, Thiry, & Melton, 2010), and are more engaged in their campuses (Kinzie, Gonyea, Shoup, & Kuh, 2008; Kuh, Kinzie, Schuh, Whitt, & Associates, 2010). Participation in

Figure 3.2. CSU Northridge Six-Year Graduation Rates by Student Ethnicity and Self-Reported Number of Participations in High-Impact Practices

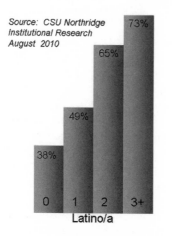

undergraduate research is also linked to academic success, retention, and persistence (Finley & McNair, 2013; Jones, Barlow, & Villarejo, 2010; Kinzie et al., 2008; Kuh et al., 2010; Russell, Hancock, & McCullough, 2007; Taraban, 2008), and these benefits are pronounced for traditionally underserved students (Finley & McNair, 2013; Osborn & Karukstis, 2009). Underrepresented minority students, students who enter college with less academic preparation, and first-generation students demonstrate the greatest benefits from undergraduate research (Finley & McNair, 2013; Kinzie et al., 2008; Lopatto, 2007).

Introducing students to research early and over time greatly increases its impact on student retention and academic performance (Jones et al., 2010) and increases the benefits of undergraduate research for all students (Bauer & Bennett, 2003). Schultz et al. (2011) found that minority students who had participated in undergraduate research experiences were more likely to persist in their intentions to pursue a research career.

Enhancing Undergraduate Research for Underrepresented Minorities Within the CSU

The Council on Undergraduate Research's *Characteristics of Excellence in Undergraduate Research* (Hensel, 2012) outlines 12 essential characteristics that enhance undergraduate research, which take on even greater importance for underrepresented, first-generation, and low-income students. Here we discuss seven characteristics that the CSU is leveraging to benefit these students.

Support Programs. The undergraduate research experience is not limited to the lab, field, library, or studio. It should include robust programming to support communication skills development, cohort and peer network development, and professional skills training (Hensel, 2012).

Hathaway, Nagda, and Gregerman (2002) found that students who participated in structured undergraduate research programs with activities such as career workshops, peer advising, and group meetings were more prepared and more likely to go on to graduate programs. More recently, the CSU Louis Stokes Alliance for Minority Participation (CSU-LSAMP), a system-wide program with the explicit goal of increasing representation of underrepresented students in STEM disciplines, surveyed 191 CSU undergraduate researchers, 70% of whom were underrepresented minorities, finding that students who engaged in support activities such as journal clubs, workshops, and field trips reported greater gains in thinking and working like a scientist. Of those engaged in additional support activities, 68% reported "a lot of gain" in "formulating a research question that could be answered with data," compared with only 46% of nonparticipants (Messier, Barker, & Nelson, 2013).

Support programs are also essential in making successful research partnerships between students and faculty. Schwartz (2012) illustrates the emotional, professional, and financial costs to faculty participating in undergraduate research, especially faculty of color who are disproportionally called on to mentor students. The most influential factors in mitigating these costs were having adequate support programs for students and institutional support for faculty.

Currently, only four CSU campuses have centralized undergraduate research offices, but there is a growing movement to consolidate support programs, allowing for coordinating services, including workshops and trainings; marketing and communication strategies; and, importantly, evaluation and tracking of undergraduate research. Campuses use innovative funding mechanisms for centralized undergraduate research offices. California State Polytechnic University, Pomona and CSU San Bernardino used CSU Student Success funding to start an office; CSU East Bay tapped into student fees; and CSU Monterey Bay (CSUMB) used a combination of direct institutional support coupled with grants and a growing endowment.

Additionally, one third of CSU campuses are creating STEM Collaboratives with support from the Helmsley Charitable Trust. These programs blend summer immersion programs, first-year experiences, and gateway courses redesigned to include interventions, such as undergraduate research, to develop dispositional learning and to close achievement gaps. STEM Collaboratives will be organized as a learning opportunity for the system, building a case for permanent, publicly funded educational structures—in effect, a new and improved status quo.

Quality Mentoring and Role Models.   Malcom et al. (2010) state "...when students interact with faculty in doing research, they benefit from their apprentice role by becoming familiar with academic and professional networks and norms" (p. 13). The opportunity to deeply engage with role models—be they professors, graduate students, or more advanced peers—allows students to identify similarities in their backgrounds, demystify the path their mentors took to their positions, and, ultimately, view themselves in those roles. Students not only learn technical and research inquiry skills from faculty mentors in their field, but they are also socialized into the profession and build important connections to serve as resources for academic support, professional references, and graduate school preparation and admissions (Hunter et al., 2006; Laursen et al., 2010). Traditionally underrepresented students benefit the most from faculty research mentorship (Finley & McNair, 2013; Kinzie et al., 2008).

CSUMB launched the Monterey Bay Regional Mentorship Alliance with the University of California, Santa Cruz's Research Mentoring Institute, and Hartnell Community College with the mission to support, sustain, and enhance faculty and graduate student mentorship at regional academic and research institutions.

Funding for Students.   The CSU-LSAMP survey (Messier et al., 2013) found that stipends or payment for undergraduate research are critical to our target demographic, with 80% of respondents indicating that a stipend was "very important" or "important" in allowing them to participate. Financial support also trumps academic credit (61% reported that academic credit was "very important" or "important"). Students who participated in summer or summer and academic year research, rather than only academic year research, reported greater gains in "thinking and working like a scientist." Thiry, Wesson, Laursen, and Hunter (2012) found that multiyear undergraduate research experiences enabled students to develop not only the intellectual skills to advance in science but also the necessary behaviors and temperament. However, they note that most funding structures do not support multiyear research experiences for undergraduates. Because many target demographic students support their own education (Malcom et al., 2010), it is imperative to fund rigorous and multiyear research opportunities.

Currently, the bulk of funding comes from federal grants. For example, CSU-LSAMP and the Department of Education's Ronald E. McNair Post-baccalaureate Achievement programs fund student research, with a range of academic support services, conference and graduate school travel, and other professional development.

Campuses are also finding creative uses for system-level funding to support students who want to participate in undergraduate research. For example, as an evaluation criterion of its CSU-funded faculty support grants, CSU East Bay includes "the direct involvement of students in the scholarly or creative process," effectively using money earmarked for one goal and making it work for two.

Finally, there are system-wide initiatives investing heavily in undergraduate research support. The CSU affinity groups, including the CSU Program for Education and Research in Biotechnology (CSUPERB) and the Council on Ocean Affairs, Science and Technology (COAST), fund student research opportunities, travel, and conference participation. The Chancellor's Office hosts meetings, subsidizes in-state travel, and supports campus-organized research competitions and conference attendance for students.

Most often, system-level support is made available to campuses by a competitive process through formal requests for proposals with application guidelines, criteria for review, and reporting requirements. A long-time exception to this competitive approach resides in the Center for Community Engagement, which provides direct annual funding to campuses for service learning, an approach that may also work well to support undergraduate research across the CSU.

Authentic Opportunities to Calibrate Knowledge.   Bandura (1977) made a strong case for the role of "performance accomplishments" in the development of self-efficacy. Given that our target demographic students perceive themselves as "outside" the academic sphere (Ovink & Veazey, 2011), we must provide authentic opportunities for students to demonstrate and calibrate their knowledge. Martinez (2009) found that when students had more ownership over their research—such as data collection and analysis—they were more enthusiastic about the research, felt a greater association with the research field, and were more likely to pursue a STEM graduate education.

The CSU hosts a system-wide Student Research Competition that celebrates and recognizes faculty–student mentored research across the disciplines. In addition, CSUPERB hosts the annual CSU Biotechnology Symposium that gathers CSU student researchers, faculty, administrators, and biotechnology professionals.

The CSU is also developing an online peer-reviewed journal of undergraduate research, *Journal of the CSU Scholar*, that will give educators and students ongoing access to system innovations. The initial editions of the journal will include submissions of the awardees from the CSU Student Research Competition and affinity group conferences. Next steps include an electronic platform and infrastructure support for the editorial board, such as faculty-assigned time and professional incentives for faculty and students to serve as reviewers.

Societal Relevance and Community Engagement.   Much as Martinez (2009) saw with ownership factoring into student learning, CUR's and CSU's research has shown that students, particularly those from underrepresented groups, also benefit from taking ownership of their learning when they connect their research to the greater good satisfying a deep-seated need to give back to their families, communities, and society.

NEW DIRECTIONS FOR HIGHER EDUCATION • DOI: 10.1002/he

For example, at San Diego State University students apply techniques of social science research to investigate food security and health issues in three San Diego neighborhoods. At CSU Los Angeles, film students use the documentary form to "put a face on critical issues impacting our nation's youth." At CSU Fresno, students work with community partners on water quality and habitat restoration, as well as teaching aquatic ecology modules in local classrooms.

Links From Community College.   The CSU system is the largest baccalaureate degree granting institution in the United States; however, over 63% of all California high school graduates admitted as freshmen in California higher education enroll at a community college, including 75% of Hispanic students. A high percentage of students who transfer to the CSU are underrepresented, but they are often unable to find timely campus resources (Moore & Shulock, 2010) and miss out on high-impact experiences (Malcom et al., 2010). CSU Fullerton (CSUF) and three local community colleges—Citrus College, Cypress College, and Santiago Canyon College—are tackling this issue head-on with funding from the Department of Education. CSUF students mentor community college students in career workshops and individually, and recruit for CSUF's Summer Research Experience program. Over two years, 57 community college students were paired with CSUF faculty for an eight-week paid summer research experience. CSUF peer advisors met with them weekly to discuss the struggles and triumphs of research. The program has had phenomenal success: 23 of the 25 first cohort participants transferred to four-year universities.

Curricular Enhancements.   Injecting research opportunities into the core curriculum engages all students in applied active learning (Malcom et al., 2010), but is particularly important for underrepresented students, who participate in such activities at lower rates than their peers. Fechheimer, Webber, and Kleiber (2011) compared students who took courses with an undergraduate research component to other students at the same institution. Even when controlling for academic preparation (SAT score), taking courses with an authentic research component was positively correlated with academic performance across classes (cumulative GPA). This relationship was strongest for students who had taken multiple courses with a research emphasis, findings that were consistent across disciplines.

CSU Channel Island's innovative Stepladder Program for Interdisciplinary Research and Learning (SPIRaL; funded by the W.M. Keck Foundation) introduces common research methods and develops analytical tools and skills in new lower division courses with increasingly sophisticated research projects integrated into middle and upper division courses. As reported on the project's website, "By introducing interdisciplinary research at the lower-division in a way that demonstrates the university's commitment to community engagement and service learning, SPIRaL will systematically develop intellectual depth and breadth in a broad spectrum of the student population and will encourage students to develop career and life

New Directions for Higher Education • DOI: 10.1002/he

goals marked by engaged curiosity, sustained passion, and civic responsibility. At the same time, the stepladder structure will cultivate expertise in the students continuing on to senior-level."

Fechheimer et al. (2011) also suggest that funding and incentives for faculty to incorporate undergraduate research in their courses would benefit students. However, the system-wide provision of faculty "seed mini-grants," while promising, does not represent a sustainable model.

Leveraging the System to Institutionalize Undergraduate Research Across the CSU

The above examples from CSU campuses dovetail with current literature and the *Characteristics of Excellence* that the Council for Undergraduate Research has identified as essential to support undergraduate research. Accelerating and spreading their adoption is one of the key roles of a system office.

Although charged formally with the implementation of law and policy, public university systems often find that their deeper influence lies in convening, communicating, and connecting. Several formal structures, including the "affinity groups" discussed above, were developed to regularly bring together faculty around topics of interest, pooling best practices and new ideas more efficiently than if the Chancellor's Office tried a more centralized hub-and-spoke approach.

In the shorter term, grant-funded activity can also spur the cross-campus collaboration that epitomizes well-functioning state systems. At times the very impermanence of these projects is a strength, drawing those who may avoid long-term commitments, and lending a sense of urgency and purpose to routine interaction. When campuses are allowed to opt in, the external impetus for activity can be remarkably valuable. For example, one third of the CSU campuses applied to join a series of workshops organized by the Council for Undergraduate Research (Malachowski, Ambos, Karukstis, & Osborn, 2010) to strategically devise ways to provide more comprehensive support for undergraduate research. The system-wide project entailed the appointment of delegates to a CSU council and participation in regularly scheduled conference calls and webinars. The opportunity to meet, trade ideas, and learn from others in a similar context was routinely cited at the top of the project evaluations. Furthermore, the ideas are more than academic: some innovations have spread to other campuses, including, most visibly, the creation of central undergraduate research offices.

Future Directions

Looking forward, the CSU system must: (a) deepen its understanding of undergraduate research's impact on retention, graduation, and career success; (b) stabilize faculty and undergraduate research funding; (c) provide reliable, consistent, and strong system-level leadership to develop and promote undergraduate research initiatives; (d) develop community college–CSU–University of California undergraduate research linkages; and (e) broaden the engagement of faculty and students in undergraduate research (e.g., more disciplines and curriculum/scaffolding).

Body of Evidence. While CSU takes pride in the availability of undergraduate research experiences for its traditionally underserved students, with the exception of LSAMP data, we have little quantitative evidence on how this intervention is impacting persistence and graduation. Much of the effort to strengthen the quantitative case for undergraduate research and its benefits for underserved student success is centrally coordinated and externally supported.

The CSU's recently developed Student Success Dashboard (Dashboard) will help us close the data gap on how high-impact practices affect student achievement as it compiles data already collected from campuses and repackages it for their decision makers. The Dashboard will also store records of student participation in high-impact practices, consistently and explicitly defined, to add detail and reliability to the gains suggested by the Northridge study (Figure 3.2). The CSU is developing more precise definitions and scales of intensity for some of the engaging pedagogies most commonly used around the system, including service learning, summer bridge programs, peer mentoring, and undergraduate research. The Dashboard will analyze if and how particular subgroups (such as majors, ethnicity groups, and community college transfers) are benefiting from these high-impact practices. To maximize the Dashboard's potential, the CSU must also include longitudinal data regarding alumni graduate studies and career paths.

Developing a Sustainable Model to Support Undergraduate Research Systematically. An unusual and sustained degree of central support has strengthened service learning across the CSU, and this provides a model for undergraduate research development. Four characteristics have made service learning work well in the CSU: (a) the Board of Trustees and system-wide Academic Senate issued formal resolutions supporting universal opportunities for service learning and community service, including the requirements for dedicated office and staff, and annual reports to the board; (b) presidents and the chancellor are aware of the support and its significance; (c) a system-wide Center for Community Engagement is charged with oversight and administration of the dedicated resources; and (d) within the requirements for commitment and reporting, campuses tailor their interventions to fit local mission, culture, and administrative structures.

Funding Faculty Engagement in Undergraduate Research. We must also address the funding model for faculty engagement in undergraduate research, putting a premium on undergraduate research within departmental policies of retention, promotion, and tenure; calculations of classroom and laboratory allocation; faculty workload; and student credit hours and degree requirements. This work won't be easy but should be facilitated by the research now underway with the Council on Undergraduate Research (Malachowski et al., 2010), Keck, Helmsley, BHEF, AAC&U, and others. The projects emphasize rigorous documentation of the benefits of undergraduate research, not only in student learning but also in cost effectiveness in the state's efforts to support more college-educated individuals.

Until we can strengthen the business case, undergraduate research—like other high-impact practices—will be relegated to the margins of the overall enterprise, relying on the goodwill of committed faculty members and enlightened administrators for essentially unpaid extra workload.

Leadership at the System Level. As service learning was a decade or so ago, undergraduate research in the CSU is poised for a more systematic approach. The faculty-led, grant-funded, and affinity-group-supported activities around the state are reaching critical mass, the kind that strikes us at the system level as primed for—in the words of this volume title—"a systems approach." CSU faculty and campus academic affairs administrators report that reliable, consistent support—both in money and high-level attention—is critical to their success. As we document and promote the case for undergraduate research as a high-impact, gap-closing practice, we advocate for a permanent undergraduate research center in the Chancellor's Office, on the same model as the Center for Community Engagement created in 1998.

References

Bandura, A. (1977). Self-efficacy: Toward a unifying theory of behavioral change. *Psychological Review, 84*(2), 191–215.

Bauer, K. W., & Bennett, J. S. (2003). Alumni perceptions used to assess undergraduate research experience. *Journal of Higher Education, 74*(2), 210–230.

California State University (CSU). (2008). *Access to Excellence Accountability Plan 2008 executive summary.* Retrieved from http://www.calstate.edu/accesstoexcellence/executive-summary.shtml

California State University (CSU). (2013). *2013 facts about the CSU.* Retrieved from http://www.calstate.edu/PA/2013Facts/enrollment-fall.shtml

Fechheimer, M., Webber, K., & Kleiber, P. B. (2011). How well do undergraduate research programs promote engagement and success of students? *CBE Life Sciences Education, 10*(2), 156–163.

Finley, A., & McNair, T. (2013). *Assessing underserved students' engagement in high-impact practices.* Washington, DC: Association of American Colleges and Universities.

Gurin, P., Nagda, B. A., & Lopez, G. E. (2004). The benefits of diversity in education for democratic citizenship. *Journal of Social Issues, 60,* 17–34.

Hathaway, R. S., Nagda, B. R. A., & Gregerman, S. R. (2002). The relationship of undergraduate research participation to graduate and professional education pursuit: An empirical study. *Journal of College Student Development, 43*(5), 614–631.

Hensel, N. (2012). *Characteristics of excellence in undergraduate research*. Washington, DC: Council on Undergraduate Research.

Hunter, A. B., Laursen, S. L., & Seymour, E. (2006). Becoming a scientist: The role of undergraduate research in students' cognitive, personal, and professional development. *Science Education*, *91*(1), 36–74.

Jones, M. T., Barlow, A. E., & Villarejo, M. (2010). Importance of undergraduate research for minority persistence and achievement in biology. *The Journal of Higher Education*, *81*(1), 82–115.

Kinzie, J., Gonyea, R., Shoup, R., & Kuh, G. D. (2008). Promoting persistence and success of underrepresented students: Lessons for teaching and learning. In J. M. Braxton (Ed.), *New Directions for Teaching and Learning: No. 115. The role of the classroom in college student persistence* (pp. 21–38). San Francisco, CA: Jossey-Bass.

Kuh, G. D., Kinzie, J., Schuh, J. H., Whitt, E. J., & Associates. (2010). *Student success in college: Creating conditions that matter*. San Francisco, CA: Jossey-Bass.

Laursen, S., Seymour, E., Hunter, A. B., Thiry, H., & Melton, G. (2010). *Undergraduate research in the sciences: Engaging students in real science*. San Francisco, CA: Jossey-Bass.

Lopatto, D. (2007). Undergraduate research experiences support science career decisions and active learning. *CBE Life Sciences Education*, *6*(4), 297–306.

Malachowski, M., Ambos, E., Karukstis, K., & Osborn, J. (2010). *Collaborative research: Transformational learning through undergraduate research: Comprehensive support for faculty, institutions, state systems and consortia* (NSF-DUE #0920275, #0920286).

Malcom, L. E., Dowd, A. C., & Yu, T. (2010). *Tapping HSI-STEM funds to improve Latina and Latino access to the STEM professions*. Los Angeles: University of Southern California.

Martinez, A. (2009, January 1). *Learning through research: How a summer undergraduate research experience informs college students' views of research and learning*. Retrieved from ProQuest LLC, EBSCOhost.

Messier, V., Barker, D., & Nelson, K. (2013). *Survey of 2012–2013 CSU-LSAMP research scholars*. Sacramento, CA: Institute for Social Research at California State University, Sacramento.

Moore, C., & Shulock, N. (2010). *Divided we fail: Improving completion and closing racial gaps in California's community colleges*. Sacramento: Institute for Higher Education Leadership and Policy, California State University, Sacramento.

Osborn, J. M., & Karukstis, K. K. (2009). The benefits of undergraduate research, scholarship, and creative activity. In M. Boyd & J. Wesemann (Eds.), *Broadening participation in undergraduate research: Fostering excellence and enhancing the impact* (pp. 41–53). Washington, DC: Council on Undergraduate Research.

Ovink, S. M., & Veazey, B. D. (2011). More than "Getting Us Through": A case study in cultural capital enrichment of underrepresented minority undergraduates. *Research in Higher Education*, *52*(4), 370–394.

Russell, S. H., Hancock, M. P., & McCullough, J. (2007). Benefits of undergraduate research experiences. *Science*, *316*(5824), 548–549.

Schultz, P. W., Hernandez, P. R., Woodcock, A., Estrada, M., Chance, R. C., Aguilar, M., & Serpe, R. T. (2011). Patching the pipeline: Reducing educational disparities in the sciences through minority training programs. *Educational Evaluation and Policy Analysis*, *33*(1), 95–114.

Schwartz, J. (2012). Faculty as undergraduate research mentors for students of color: Taking into account the costs. *Science Education*, *96*(3), 527–542.

Taraban, R. M. (2008). *Creating effective undergraduate research programs in science: The transformation from student to scientist*. New York, NY: Teachers College Press.

Thiry, H., Wesson, T. J., Laursen, S. L., & Hunter, A. B. (2012). The benefits of multi-year research experiences: Differences in novice and experienced students' reported gains from undergraduate research. *CBE Life Sciences Education, 11*(3), 260–272.

KEN O'DONNELL *is the senior director of Student Engagement and Academic Initiatives & Partnerships, California State University Office of the Chancellor.*

JUDY BOTELHO *is the director of the CSU Center for Community Engagement, California State University Office of the Chancellor.*

JESSICA BROWN *is the associate director of the Undergraduate Research Opportunities Center, California State University, Monterey Bay.*

GERARDO M. GONZÁLEZ *is a professor of psychology and former dean of graduate studies and associate vice president for research, California State University, San Marcos.*

WILLIAM HEAD *is the director of the Undergraduate Research Opportunities Center and a professor in the Division of Science and Environmental Policy, California State University, Monterey Bay.*

NEW DIRECTIONS FOR HIGHER EDUCATION • DOI: 10.1002/he

4

This chapter presents the state of Wisconsin and the University of Wisconsin System as an ongoing case study for best practices in systematic, intentional, statewide programming and initiatives connecting undergraduate research and economic development.

Undergraduate Research and Economic Development: A Systems Approach in Wisconsin

Dean Van Galen, Lissa Schneider-Rebozo, Karen Havholm, Kris Andrews

What relationship is there, or should there be, between undergraduate research (UR) and economic development? Until recently, relatively few faculty, administrators, or students have given much thought to this question. Those who do would point out that UR translates to economic development by preparing college graduates whose newly enhanced critical-thinking and problem-solving skills enable them to navigate the territory that connects basic research to the commercial and creative development of products, technologies, and services. There is considerable anecdotal evidence and some data showing that UR students share higher rates of retention, graduation, and future success as employees, entrepreneurs, and leaders; they often become, in a word, *innovators*. A body of evidence now exists showing the strongly positive correlation between higher education and both workforce development and the regional impact of a university as itself a business or industry (Kelly & McNicoll, 2009; Leslie & Brinkman, 1988; Weibl, Comedy, & Malcom, 2013). However, comprehensive, longitudinal studies are only now being launched that will fully assess the corollaries between UR and economic development in the form of innovation, new business creation, new technologies, and the transfer of this knowledge to host economies. Although UR has been around for years, the nationwide drive in postsecondary education to systematically and coherently implement high-impact experiences like UR is a relatively recent phenomenon—and the interest in relating UR to state and national economic development is even more recent (Business Higher Education Forum [BHEF], 2013; Shaffer & Wright, 2010).

New Directions for Higher Education, no. 169, Spring 2015 © 2015 Wiley Periodicals, Inc.
Published online in Wiley Online Library (wileyonlinelibrary.com) • DOI: 10.1002/he.20121

Although this chapter presents the state of Wisconsin and the University of Wisconsin System as an ongoing case study for connecting UR and economic development, the focus is relevant to all U.S. public higher educational institutions because all are governed and supported within a state context. Moreover, both public and private institutions of higher education are being asked to participate in the economic development of the regions that they serve (Shaffer & Wright, 2010; Weibl et al., 2013).

Economic Development as a New Imperative for Higher Education

Based on a survey of state legislative activities throughout the United States, the American Association of State Colleges and Universities cited "Harnessing Higher Education to Address State Economic Goals" as the leading higher education issue for 2014 (Hurley, Harnisch, & Parker, 2014, p. 2). In part, this new legislative focus reflects the pressure on public policy makers and political leaders to catalyze economic development and job creation. Universities and colleges have long pointed out that attaining a college degree leads to positive outcomes for graduates. Recently, data compiled by the Pew Research Center showed that annual earnings trended strongly higher and unemployment rates dramatically declined with higher education (Caumont, 2014). However, in today's environment, a university's affirmative roles in both workforce development and in local/regional/state impact (i.e., the university as a business or industry) are seen as roles that fulfill only part of a university's full potential to support economic development.

Higher education is now expected to do more than produce well-educated, career-ready graduates. Today, expectations often include producing graduates in high-need areas, providing expertise to the private sector, engaging in university–business partnerships, technology transfer, and new business creation. While these activities are elements of the historic missions of major research universities (Blank, 2014), expectations are now being extended to all sectors of higher education, including comprehensive universities and community colleges.

The Wisconsin Story: State-Level Strategies to Connect Undergraduate Research and Economic Development

The University of Wisconsin (UW) System is composed of a diverse set of institutions serving approximately 180,000 students. Governed by a single 18-member Board of Regents, the system includes a world-class research institution (UW-Madison), an urban research university (UW-Milwaukee), 11 comprehensive universities, 13 freshman/sophomore colleges, and UW-Extension. In the state of Wisconsin, economic development programs with ties to the UW System and UR are numerous and diverse. What follows is a

NEW DIRECTIONS FOR HIGHER EDUCATION • DOI: 10.1002/he

brief discussion of Wisconsin's long tradition of distinction in UR together with a description of key state and UW-System-level strategies, policy decisions, and commitments to UR and its potential for promoting economic development.

Undergraduate Research in the UW System: A Historical Overview. UR has an especially long and vibrant history in the UW System that can be traced back to the 1960s. With a few notable exceptions, most UR across the system emerged organically through the leadership of individual faculty members in the academic departments. At UW-Eau Claire, the chemistry and history departments proved to be among the most active early participants in UR, with Eau Claire's chemistry department producing its first coauthored faculty/undergraduate scholarly publication in 1960 (Collins, Goethel, & Hei, 1960), while history's discipline-specific UR requirement, at this writing, approaches its 50th anniversary. In 1963, at UW-River Falls, sociology professor Robert Bailey developed a multidisciplinary UR program meeting definitional criteria (i.e., a program designed to foster intentional, faculty-mentored, student- or faculty-initiated original UR). The program, Quarter/Semester Abroad Europe, is still going strong today. The original inclusive vision combined two "high-impact" practices (to use today's terminology; Kuh, 2008), UR and global learning, as a means of helping all students, and especially those from underrepresented groups, to achieve intellectual and economic success (Bailey, 1991). Bailey's model anticipates many of the current efforts being spearheaded in the UW System, which are blending UR and other high-impact practices like internships with increasing intentionality. With these programs, the goal is to positively contribute to long-standing state priorities (retention, graduation rates, workforce development), as well as to the current emphasis on innovation and knowledge transfer.

The first wave of centralization and organization around UR in the UW System occurred in the late 1980s. In 1988, UW-Eau Claire applied for and received certification from UW System as a "Center of Excellence for Faculty and Undergraduate Student Research Collaboration." With that designation and the funding it provided, UW-Eau Claire began offering research support for its undergraduates. In 1999, UW-Milwaukee developed a UR program operating within a larger retention initiative called the Edison Initiative; this was preceded earlier in 1999 with UW-Madison's program, which follows a similar model. One year earlier, UW-Whitewater was the first to hire a dedicated UR director in 1998. Today, campus-based centralized offices have emerged across the UW System, especially at the comprehensives, in a movement strongly propelled forward by participation in the 2010 Council on Undergraduate Research's (CUR) competitive program for systems and consortia (Malachowski, Ambos, Karukstis, & Osborn, 2010). In 2014, the Wisconsin System Council on Undergraduate Research (WiSCUR) was formed in an effort to increase access to and ensure quality of the UR experience at each UW System institution.

Commitment of the UW System Governing Board. In collaboration with the UW System president, campus chancellors, and business leaders, the UW System Board of Regents has taken action to emphasize and support the role of UR in economic development. In 2012, the Board of Regents established the Research, Economic Development and Innovation (REDI) Committee comprised of nine regents. UR has been a major focus of the REDI Committee's efforts to implement best practices, incentivize and reward faculty, and collaborate with the Wisconsin Economic Development Corporation on Wisconsin's economic development priorities (Horn, 2013). In 2013, the REDI Committee gained full Board of Regents approval for a five-year, $1 million annual commitment to support the WiSys Technology Foundation. These funds support research and technology transfer at UW's two-year and four-year primarily undergraduate campuses, and thereby directly support UR. In 2014, the board approved an additional $1 million investment for two programs: "Undergraduate Research and Discovery Grants" and a "Regent Scholar Program." The former provides "capacity building" grants to each of the system's 26 institutions to support UR, while the latter establishes five $50,000 competitive awards for faculty to be named "Regent Scholars." Regent Scholars will be selected by public and private sector experts and will use the awards for UR. Both programs are designed to encourage participation by underrepresented faculty and students in UR, close achievement gaps in student success and completion, and spur regional economic development. In Wisconsin, the symbolic and tangible leadership demonstrated by the UW Board of Regents has strengthened UR and encouraged connections with economic development.

Wisconsin State Funding Strategies. As part of the approved 2013–2015 state budget, the UW System allocated $22.5 million to launch the Economic Development Incentive Grant Program. For this program, UW System institutions submitted proposals that aligned with one or more of the following three categories: (a) economic development activities, (b) development of an educated and skilled workforce, and/or (c) improve affordability of postsecondary higher education. Projects that could be shown to positively impact traditional and emerging Wisconsin industries and advance new educational and research initiatives were privileged in a competitive review process conducted by business and higher education leaders. Twelve winners were selected from a field of 78 applicants, and many of the funded projects include a strong element of UR. Funded projects focus on research in aquaponics and aquaculture, engineering technology, and geological advances to support sustainable mining technology, among others that will be discussed later in this chapter. Additional funding for these projects attracted $4.5 million in private sector match grants and in-kind support.

University-Related Technology Transfer Corporations. The National Science Foundation's National Center for Science and Engineering

Statistics reports that higher education research and development expenditures in Wisconsin exceeded $1.4 billion in fiscal year 2012 (National Center for Science and Engineering Statistics, 2014). In addition, academic research funding, patent filings, and other technology transfer metrics in Wisconsin "overperform" for the state population (Wisconsin Growth Capital Coalition, 2011, p. 3). Wisconsin benefits from a strong support structure for university-related technology transfer through three nonprofit corporations developed for this purpose.

Founded in 1925, the Wisconsin Alumni Research Foundation (WARF) is the private, nonprofit patent and licensing organization for UW-Madison. WARF's inception traces back to the discovery of a pioneering process to fortify vitamin D content in food; today, WARF manages a $2 billion endowment and has obtained 1,900 U.S. patents and more than 1,600 licensing agreements. In 2006, UW-Milwaukee established its own research foundation to serve a similar purpose.

In 2000, the WiSys Technology Foundation (WiSys) was established to support innovation and technology transfer at the 11 comprehensive and 13 two-year campuses in the UW System. From its inception, engaging undergraduate students in research has been an important element of WiSys activity, with $7.9 million in UR investment as part of its material assistance to projects that have a high potential for commercialization. To date, WiSys support has resulted in 14 startup companies. Many of these startups have been supported directly or indirectly by undergraduate researchers.

Wisconsin Small Business Development Centers and Specialty Centers: 35 Years and Still Innovating. In 1979, both UW-Madison and UW-Eau Claire established Small Business Development Centers (SBDCs) as part of an emerging statewide network of SBDCs working with business owners and entrepreneurs to facilitate business growth and improvement, to mobilize university resources, and to launch successful new companies. The idea for a statewide SBDC network—allowing ready regional access to all state citizens while deploying university resources to promote the public good and improve the lives of our citizens beyond the classroom—is philosophically linked to what is known as "The Wisconsin Idea" in education, an idea first attributed to UW-Madison President Charles Van Hise in 1904. In this spirit, through no-cost consulting, low-cost entrepreneurial education, and strategic facilitation, SBDC Wisconsin experts, often with undergraduate and graduate student support and involvement, serve as resources for small and emerging mid-size companies.

Today UW-Eau Claire and UW-Madison's SBDCs continue to operate in collaboration with other statewide SBDCs with ties to the four-year campuses at Green Bay, La Crosse, Milwaukee, Oshkosh, Parkside, Platteville, River Falls, Steven's Point, Superior, and Whitewater. The regional SBDC programs are being joined by new specialty centers, increasing opportunities for outreach, innovation, and public/private collaborations with local corporations, with the intent of promoting steady growth of existing businesses as well as providing sustained structures for systematically encouraging and nurturing entrepreneurial innovation among our students and within our business communities.

Specialty Centers. Wisconsin Specialty Centers work with cocurricular programming to connect UW classrooms with applied corporate research and development projects. Three different models include (a) the UW-River Falls (UWRF) Center for Innovation and Business Development (CIBD) in River Falls, which opened in May 2014; (b) the Discovery Center in Stout (2009); and (c) the Alta Resources Center for Entrepreneurship and Innovation (CEI) at Oshkosh (2014).

The new CIBD, in a partnership with UWRF's Summer Internship and Entrepreneurship program, offers an interesting case study with two notable features in its pilot phase. In its first summer iteration, four local businesses with strong national and international markets are working together to sponsor 15 undergraduate summer internships. The research-intensive internships blend features of each high-impact practice to allow undergraduates to work directly on the applied design and development phases of new products intended for market. The second notable feature of the program involves the establishment of "Innovation Fellows": PhD-level corporate researchers who will teach classes at UWRF and who, by virtue of their combined work/R&D experience, provide the critical links connecting basic scientific research and undergraduate classroom activities with practical entrepreneurial applications and real market forces.

At Stout, the Discovery Center, together with its offshoots like the Sustainability Sciences Institute (SSI), uses a different model to advance the UW's educational mission while providing solutions to business and industry challenges. Since 2009, the Discovery Center has facilitated dozens of collaborative projects involving cross-disciplinary teams of more than 300 students and faculty. These projects tap resources from every college on campus and connect UW-Stout with industry and community partners that enable student participation in applied research and development.

The UW-Oshkosh CEI specialty center, still in its pilot phase, remains wholly focused on encouraging students to pursue career and business development ideas. The CEI has opened the Student Business Design Lab, a collaborative student space with an architectural plan uniquely intended to marry form and function as a means of generating new product and business ideas. The CEI also offers up to 12 team-building opportunities and competitions for UW-Oshkosh undergraduates from various colleges and disciplines. While the university/business partnership is a possible model for public–private initiatives that may lead to job creation and economic growth for the CEI, which receives some funding and expertise from the Wisconsin Economic Development Corporation (WEDC), the core mission remains educational (Alta Resources, UW Oshkosh College of Business Partner in Center for Entrepreneurship and Innovation, 2014).

Applied Undergraduate Research and Economical Fee-for-Service Models: UW-La Crosse's Statistical Consulting Center and UW-Eau Claire's Materials Science Center.   The Wisconsin SBDCs generally follow an incubator model to nurture the successful development of startups and the growth of existing small and mid-size businesses. Some of the SBDC-affiliated incubators are geared wholly toward the needs of entrepreneurial students: for example, UW-Madison's Student Business Incubator and UW-Oshkosh's CEI (Tempus, 2009). In the incubator models in the UW System, undergraduate researchers with startup ideas may be on the receiving end for office space, business advice, legal guidance, and professional services. Conversely, undergraduate researchers who are seeking cooperative work experiences and real-world problem-solving challenges may be recruited to work (under a mentor's direction) on the service side to provide new or fledgling regional businesses with professional services or research skills. At UW-La Crosse, the Statistical Consulting Center (SCC) recruits undergraduate statistics majors to work in the latter capacity. The SCC's operations serve the dual agendas of regional economic development and workforce development in a win–win combination that benefits the community and the UW-La Crosse student researchers in equal measure.

The fee for analytical services model of La Crosse's SCC is also used by UW-Eau Claire's Materials Science Center (MSC), which provides its student researchers with state-of-the-art equipment and methodologies, while they and their faculty mentors help companies to solve their materials-related problems. The MSC currently works with about 20 companies per year on production method development and troubleshooting, reverse engineering, quality assurance, materials characterization in products and in the waste stream, confirmation of correct functionality of industrial processes and monitoring the process for wear of components, and causal analyses in cases of product or process failure. MSC analyses have resulted in large savings for the companies involved; it has built a strong reputation as an industrial partner, a nexus of educational resources for K–12 institutions, and a rigorous campus program for training undergraduate researchers.

UW-Madison's D2P: The Accelerator Model for Economic Development.   The accelerator model for promoting economic development differs from incubators in that accelerator programs generally make an investment in the companies they enroll, and provide more intensive levels of mentorship. Thus, the overall goal of incubators and accelerators remains the same—to facilitate startups and encourage economic development—while going about it in different ways (Chan, 2014). UW-Madison's Discovery to Product program (D2P) follows the accelerator model to cultivate entrepreneurship, secure intellectual property, accelerate transfer of campus innovations, and systematically make possible optimal conditions for technology transfer (Mattmiller, 2013). Like UW-La Crosse's Statistical Consulting Center, Madison's D2P is a recipient of a 2013–15 UW System Economic Development Incentive grant. D2P, in a partnership with WARF, supports two pools of activity, with funding and strongly mentored support for up to 10 projects in an accelerated pool, and 25 other precompany innovations in a second, unfunded pool. Graduation from the accelerated pool occurs upon licensing or incorporation and equity funding, while movement into the accelerated pool ensues on achievement of some significant external funding (Engel, 2014). All UW-Madison students, faculty, and staff with a new product or business idea are eligible to apply (DeLuca & Cook, 2014).

Cocurricular Programming and Economic Development: UW-Milwaukee's Startup Challenge.   Many of the programs discussed in this chapter utilize a cocurricular approach to UR. UW-Milwaukee's Startup Challenge, funded in 2012 by the National Collegiate Inventors and Innovators Alliance (NCIIA) and the UW System's Growth Agenda for Wisconsin, presents itself as a contest rather than a grant competition and exclusively supports cocurricular student research and entrepreneurship, with eligibility for all UW-Milwaukee current students and alumni who have graduated within the last two years (Shafer, 2013). Like UW-Madison's D2P, the Startup Challenge provides award monies and mentorship for up to 10 innovative ideas a year, and, also like D2P, it is multidisciplinary and broad-based in the scope of the projects it is willing and able to support. It differs from D2P in its emphasis on students and the educational mission, which allows for a somewhat longer view of economic impact and development outcomes. Thus, cofounder Brian Thompson uses a classic workforce development argument when he explains that undergraduates who participate in the Startup Challenge are learning entrepreneurial skills that they will apply to future endeavors, regardless of the ultimate dispensation of particular Startup Challenge projects. One of the Startup Challenge's more striking features is the congruence between its origins and its educational mission: in other words, this cocurricular program that espouses experiential learning and cocreation is itself the dynamic product of experiential learning, cocreation, and ongoing collaboration between faculty and administrators. Winning ideas are intended to form the basis of new products and companies. The program helps student entrepreneurs build a team, develop working prototypes, form and launch a company as a legal entity, and develop an investor-ready business plan (Romell, 2012).

Klesse and D'Onofrio (2000) have argued that "cocurricular pursuits enhance the educational program by providing additional benefits not derived from classroom activities" (pp. 5–8). This is the belief that underwrites the movement toward all cocurricular programming associated with UW System campuses, including those that align with UR and economic development initiatives.

Conclusions

In the University of Wisconsin System, the case for the economic value of UR has already been made, and won, at least for now. Consequently, in the last three years, we have seen statewide implementation of new programming designed to systematically and coherently produce conditions for UR—and especially for UR as it relates to technology transfer, job creation, and new/expanding industries and businesses. In this chapter, we are reporting on some of the state support structures and recent key policy and program initiatives that specially relate to economic development. These have been discussed in context within an already flourishing UW System UR movement and the established positive correlation between UR and the development of a skilled and committed workforce.

While we have seen strong initial success, it will be especially important to track and assess outcomes for these new initiatives, and the development of meaningful assessment structures is almost as great a challenge to design and implement as the new UR/economic development programs themselves. Recognizing this imperative for follow-up, WiSCUR has set up five initial task forces—one of these is devoted to economic development, another to assessment/data tracking. While there are many more new and existing initiatives in our state and system to discuss than space here allows, we have presented an overview of the intentional, sustained UR/economic development activity in Wisconsin, and we hope that it offers a useful narrative and template that may help others.

References

Alta Resources, UW Oshkosh College of Business Partner in Center for Entrepreneurship and Innovation. (2014, April 30). *UW Oshkosh Today*. Retrieved from http://www.uwosh.edu/today/33326/alta-resources-pledges-funding-resources-to-uw-oshkosh-college-of-business-center-for-entrepreneurship-and-innovation/

Bailey, R. B., III. (1991). The River Falls experience: Custom-designing study abroad. In J. Booth (Ed.), *Black students and overseas programs* (pp. 21–29). Council on International Educational Exchange (CIEE). Retrieved from http://www.ciee.org/research_center/archive/CIEE_Education_Abroad_Informational_Documents/1991BlackStudentsOverseas.pdf

Blank, B. (2014, March 21). *Why we need to strengthen our economic development efforts.* University of Wisconsin Madison: Office of the Chancellor. Retrieved from http://www.chancellor.wisc.edu/blog/why-we-need-to-strengthen-our-economic-development-efforts/

Business Higher Education Forum (BHEF). (2013). *The national higher education and workforce initiative: Forging strategic partnerships for undergraduate innovation and workforce development. BHEF 2013 Playbook.* Washington, DC: Author. Retrieved from http://www.bhef.com/sites/g/files/g829556/f/201308/2013_report_playbook.PDF

Caumont, A. (2014, February 11). 6 key findings about going to college. *Pew Research Center FACTANK.* Retrieved from http://www.pewresearch.org/fact-tank/2014/02/11/6-key-findings-about-going-to-college/

Chan, K. (2014, February 24). Incubator vs. accelerator—What's the difference? *Oxbridge Biotech Roundtable.* Retrieved from http://www.oxbridgebiotech.com/review/business-development/incubator-vs-accelerator-whats-difference/

Collins, J. O., Goethel, W. R., & Hei, J. O. (1960, January). Determination of di-o-tolylguanidine dicatechol borate in rubber compounds. *Rubber Chemistry and Technology, 33*(1), 237–239.

NEW DIRECTIONS FOR HIGHER EDUCATION • DOI: 10.1002/he

DeLuca, P. M., Jr., & Cook, M. E. (2014, February 6). *Discovery to product (D2P) and igniter: Revving the start-up engine at UW-Madison.* University of Wisconsin System Board of Regents. Retrieved from http://www.uwsa.edu/bor/agenda/2014/february-redi.pdf

Engel, J. (2014, April 11). D2P's Biondi on getting UW-Madison more for its ($1.2B) R&D money. *Xconomy.* Retrieved from http://www.xconomy.com/wisconsin/2014/04/11/d2ps-biondi-on-getting-uw-madison-more-for-its-1-2b-rd-money/

Horn, O. (2013, December). *Translating talent and research into new discoveries and jobs.* University of Wisconsin System Office of Economic Development progress report. Retrieved from https://www.wisconsin.edu/economic-development/2014/07/08/translating-talent-and-research-into-new-discoveries-and-jobs/

Hurley, D. J., Harnisch, T. L., & Parker, E. A. (2014, January). Top 10 higher education state policy issues for 2014. *AASCU PolicyMatters: A Higher Education Policy Brief.* Retrieved from http://www.aascu.org/policy/publications/policy-matters/Top10State PolicyIssues2014.pdf

Kelly, U., & McNicoll, I. (2009, June). Outputs and outcomes: Quantifying the impact of higher education institutions. *Impact of higher education institutions on regional economies: A joint research initiative.* Cambridge University. Retrieved from http://www.cbr.cam.ac.uk/pdf/UKirc_Wksp_4-5Jun_Presentations/session_5_ursula_Kelly_outputs_and~_outcomes.pdf

Klesse, E. J., & D'Onofrio, J. A. (2000, October). The value of cocurricular activities. *NASSP.* Retrieved from https://www.nassp.org/portals/0/content/48943.pdf

Kuh, G. D. (2008). *High-impact educational practices: What they are, who has access to them, and why they matter.* Washington, DC: American Association of Colleges and Universities.

Leslie, L. L., & Brinkman, P. T. (1988). *The economic value of higher education* (The American Council on Education/Macmillan Series ed.). New York, NY: Macmillan.

Malachowski, M., Ambos, E., Karukstis, K., & Osborn, J. (2010). *Collaborative research: Transformational learning through undergraduate research: Comprehensive support for faculty, institutions, state systems and consortia* (NSF-DUE #0920275, #0920286).

Mattmiller, B. (2013, December 3). *New advocacy group focuses on kick-starting UW business creation.* University of Wisconsin Madison: News. Retrieved from http://www.news.wisc.edu/22364

National Center for Science and Engineering Statistics. (2014, February). *Higher education research and development survey: Fiscal year 2012.* National Science Foundation. Retrieved from http://ncsesdata.nsf.gov/herd/2012/

Romell, R. (2012, October 6). UWM start-up contest throws cash behind entrepreneurs' ideas. *Journal Sentinel.* Retrieved from http://www.jsonline.com/business/uwm-startup-contest-throws-cash-behind-entrepreneurs-ideas-n0722kk-172903231.html

Shafer, D. (2013, December 23). UWM program aims to create entrepreneurial students. *BizTimes.com.* Retrieved from http://www.biztimes.com/article/20131223/MAGAZINE03/312139986/0/magazine02/UWM-program-aims-to-create-entrepreneurial-students

Shaffer, D. F., & Wright, D. J. (2010, March). A new paradigm for economic development: How higher education institutions are working to revitalize their regional and state economies. *Higher Education: The Public Policy Research Arm of the State University of New York.* Retrieved from http://www.rockinst.org/pdf/education/2010-03-18-A_New_Paradigm.pdf

Tempus, A. (2009, February). Business incubator sparks ideas. *The Badger Herald.* Retrieved from http://badgerherald.com/news/2009/02/12/business-incubator-s/#.U6dqwsacOa4

Weibl, R. A., Comedy, Y. L., & Malcom, S. M. (2013). *Education and workforce development in the FY 2014 budget.* American Association for the Advancement of Science. Retrieved from http://www.aaas.org/sites/default/files/RnD/FY2014/14pch04.pdf

Wisconsin Growth Capital Coalition. (2011, September). *Building companies and jobs: The case for a venture capital program in Wisconsin.* Wisconsin Technology Council. Retrieved from http://www.wisconsintechnologycouncil.com/uploads/WGCC _BuildlingCompanies_final.pdf

DEAN VAN GALEN *is the chancellor of the UW-River Falls and serves on the WiSys Technology Foundation Board of Trustees.*

LISSA SCHNEIDER-REBOZO *is the director of Undergraduate Research, Scholarly, and Creative Activity and associate professor of English at UW-River Falls.*

KAREN HAVHOLM *is assistant vice chancellor for Research and Sponsored Programs and director of the Center of Excellence for Faculty and Undergraduate Student Research Collaboration at UW-Eau Claire.*

KRIS ANDREWS *is the vice president for Federal Relations at the UW System.*

5

This chapter delineates the consortial activities of the Council of Public Liberal Arts Colleges (COPLAC) to explore models of undergraduate research and to address the impact of undergraduate research on faculty workload. The significant progress made on the member campus of the University of Wisconsin-Superior over the last 10 years is highlighted as an example of the fortuitous impact of several concurrent factors in advancing undergraduate research.

Faculty Workload Issues Connected to Undergraduate Research

Rhona Free, Suzanne Griffith, Bill Spellman

Established in 1987 and now consisting of 28 colleges and universities in 26 states and one Canadian province, the Council of Public Liberal Arts Colleges (COPLAC) represents a small but unique sector in postsecondary education. Member campuses strive to emulate the best teaching and learning practices of North America's private liberal arts institutions. With small classes, a strong arts and sciences core, innovative curricula, and close faculty–student interactions, COPLAC institutions seek to combine an egalitarian concern for access to the liberal arts experience with academic rigor, including opportunities for independent research and creative activity.

Early Steps to Advance COPLAC's Culture of Undergraduate Research

A 2010 consortium-wide survey of high-impact practices (HIPs) identified undergraduate research (UR) as a major academic priority for COPLAC member institutions. Encouraged by this finding, campus leaders began collectively to examine the scope, output, and level of administrative support for UR activity. In collaboration with COPLAC's administrative office, faculty stakeholders began discussing the possibility of sharing best practices and leveraging the size of the consortium to expand opportunities for student researchers.

Early discussions focused on the workload implications of one-on-one mentoring of UR. Typically the smallest and most teaching-intensive

NEW DIRECTIONS FOR HIGHER EDUCATION, no. 169, Spring 2015 © 2015 Wiley Periodicals, Inc.
Published online in Wiley Online Library (wileyonlinelibrary.com) • DOI: 10.1002/he.20122

campus within their respective state systems, COPLAC member institutions must make difficult choices when reductions in system-wide operating budgets threaten the academic core. Given these hard choices, how can the work of mentoring undergraduate researchers be factored into teaching load? How might faculty members at COPLAC institutions avoid overspecialization and claim UR mentoring as a mark of professional success at primarily undergraduate institutions? How can our consortium refine the faculty rewards system to include the widely recognized "high-impact" value of UR on student learning?

In late 2010, our efforts to answer these questions intersected nicely with a CUR Workshop Program on Institutionalizing Undergraduate Research for State Systems and Consortia (Malachowski, Ambos, Karukstis, & Osborn, 2010). The June 2011 workshop enabled us to bring together almost 100 faculty members from 23 member campuses for three days of structured discussions, formal presentations, and informal sharing of successes and failures. Led by 12 CUR facilitators, participants explored models for UR that would be most appropriate for small- to medium-size public liberal arts colleges and universities. Recognizing a considerable range of administrative practice involving UR on member campuses, team leaders agreed to develop campus action plans for the 2011–2012 academic year, share their reports at a CUR-led follow-up workshop in June 2012, and set new campus goals while also building capacity for future collaborations.

The 2012 team leader workshop was held in conjunction with COPLAC's Annual Meeting. To maintain momentum after the conclusion of the CUR grant, COPLAC entered into conversations with the Association of American Colleges and Universities (AAC&U) and was recognized as an official partner in the LEAP States Initiative, with a special focus on continuous improvement in UR. A "LEAP Project" link was added to the COPLAC website, and member campuses began providing regular updates on their UR activities.

Partly on the strength of our CUR workshop efforts, COPLAC received a two-year grant from the Teagle Foundation under a "Faculty Work and Student Learning in the 21st Century" initiative. Specifically, COPLAC was funded to develop a pilot project for distance mentoring of UR with the goal of making available to student researchers the disciplinary expertise of faculty members from across the consortium. With more than two dozen campuses and over 4,500 full-time faculty members consortium-wide, a successful model for distance mentoring of UR had the potential to open up multiple areas of disciplinary expertise that are not available to undergraduate researchers at small- to medium-sized public liberal arts colleges.

Over the course of three semesters, the distance mentoring pilot project engaged 32 student researchers and 23 faculty mentors from 15 COPLAC campuses. Qualitative assessments indicate that student and faculty participants highly valued their distance partnerships, and the gains reported by these students corresponded to those experienced by traditionally mentored students. The program also provided a faculty development opportunity through working with strong students in an area of the mentor's interests and through developing expertise with the technologies needed to support close collaboration at a distance. The Teagle grant concluded in July 2014, but the overall success of the pilot led COPLAC'S board in June 2014 to create a budget line to continue distance mentoring of UR on a permanent basis.

In addition to testing the viability of distance mentored UR and assessing its impact on student learning, the Teagle grant enabled COPLAC to explore new ways of defining credit-bearing courses, the shape of faculty work in an increasingly constrained fiscal environment, and the larger faculty rewards system. A steering committee was established consisting of UR directors, faculty mentors, academic deans, and chief academic officers. Meeting biannually, the committee developed a set of best practices for recognizing and rewarding faculty work in UR mentoring. The recommendations included a call for member campuses to create formal, clearly articulated procedures for rewarding mentors in promotion, tenure, and renewal decisions; encouraged the establishment of written criteria for merit pay (when available); endorsed a credit-banking system for faculty mentors; and supported the development of strategies for embedding UR in courses that are part of a faculty member's normal teaching load. During its discussions, the committee was respectful of individual campus cultures and state-specific rules on faculty work while still moving toward a broad COPLAC standard to account for and reward one-on-one mentoring.

National Trends and COPLAC Practice

At most regional public colleges and universities, UR or creative activity is not an integral element of the curriculum or institutional marketing and branding strategies, and faculty course loads are high. The average faculty load at COPLAC schools is 12 credit hours per semester, corresponding to an average four-course load and 12 contact hours of course meetings a week. UR mentoring is challenging with the standard COPLAC course load. Many excellent publications describe approaches to incorporating UR into the curriculum (Gates, Teller, Bernat, Delgado, & Della-Piana, 1999; Reinen, Grasfils, Gaines, & Hazlett, 2007; Temple, Sibley, & Orr, 2010), and a few (Hakim, 2000; Kierniesky, 2005; Merkel, 2001; Pukkila, DeCosmo, Swick, & Arnold, 2007; Rueckert, 2007) also address how faculty are compensated for mentoring that work, how mentoring affects their workload, or how mentoring is addressed in promotion and tenure.

In order to assess the prevalence of UR at public liberal arts colleges with greater emphasis on teaching, how it is incorporated in the curriculum, how faculty are compensated for mentoring undergraduate researchers, and how this work is addressed in promotion and tenure, a survey was sent in fall 2013 to COPLAC institutions, yielding 16 responses (14 responses were

Table 5.1. Faculty and Student Participation in Undergraduate Research at COPLAC Institutions

Percentage of Faculty Mentoring UR on a Regular Basis in a One-on-One or Small Group Environment	Number of Campuses	Percentage of Students Participating in UR on a Regular Basis in a One-on-One or Small Group Environment	Number of Campuses
> 80	2		
61–79	0	51–60	2
51–60	3	25–50	2
26–50	5	10–25	8
≤25	6	<10	4

complete). Table 5.1 indicates that, at the majority of campuses responding to the survey, less than 50% of faculty mentor UR on a regular basis in a one-on-one or small group environment, and 25% or less of the students participate in UR in these forms. These figures suggest that while COPLAC institutions are committed to the personalized high-impact learning provided by UR, the experience is still not shared by a majority of students or faculty at most of the schools, possibly because UR does not fit neatly into the curriculum or faculty workload. Results from this survey are consistent with results from the National Survey of Student Engagement (NSSE). Among seniors at COPLAC institutions who responded to the 2012 NSSE, 36% said that they had or planned to "Work on a research project with a faculty member outside of course or program requirements." This compared to 34% of all seniors responding to the 2012 NSSE.

Where does UR fit into the curriculum at COPLAC schools? Tables 5.2 and 5.3 summarize the survey results. At most COPLAC schools, UR can be offered through independent studies, summer research projects, small research seminars, or embedded within a course (Table 5.2). Table 5.3, however, shows that while a number of methods may be available, there are only four campuses where a majority of students completed UR during the academic year in a credit-bearing course with multiple students as part of faculty member's regular teaching load.

Table 5.2. Method of Incorporating Undergraduate Research in the Curriculum at COPLAC Institutions

Method of Conducting UR	Number of Campuses
Independent studies	16
Summer research projects	16
Small research seminars	15
Embedded within a course	14
Other models	5

Table 5.3. Timing of Undergraduate Research at COPLAC Institutions

Timing of UR	Number of Campuses
Primarily during the academic year in a credit-bearing course with multiple students as part of faculty member's regular teaching load	4
Primarily during the academic year in credit-bearing independent studies	3
Primarily during the summer in a credit-bearing course with multiple students	1
Primarily during the summer in credit-bearing independent study courses	2
No dominant mode	5

Faculty members' compensation incorporates responsibility for mentoring UR when it is part of a faculty member's regular teaching load, but that is not the case with other formats. On most COPLAC campuses faculty members do not get load credit for supervising independent study during the academic year, and they are not compensated in another way. Most campuses do not allow faculty members to "bank" credits accrued for teaching independent studies (see Paul [2012] for a detailed discussion of how this works). At 10 of 15 COPLAC campuses responding, faculty members are compensated for UR mentoring during the summer. At a January 2014 meeting of chief academic officers from COPLAC institutions that participated in the CUR initiative (Malachowski et al., 2010), there was strong consensus that although there may be indirect benefits to faculty for mentoring, providing direct benefits in the form of pay or load credit is essential to ensuring continued faculty participation.

Is the willingness of COPLAC faculty to mentor UR even without direct compensation a result of strong rewards for it in the promotion and tenure process? At a majority of COPLAC campuses, mentoring of UR is considered informally in evaluations including those for renewal, promotion, tenure, and merit pay. It is considered formally most often in promotion decisions, but even then this is the case at only 25% of responding campuses. At one campus it is formally considered in renewal, at three for tenure, at four for promotion, at two for annual reviews, and at two for merit pay. At one campus where it is considered formally, consideration is given for the supervision and mentoring of UR or creative endeavors. At another the union contract states that teaching effectiveness, including independent studies, shall be used in the evaluation of all full-time faculty members.

Unless there are formal procedures for rewarding UR in promotion, tenure, and renewal or strong evidence that faculty benefit in the form of increased scholarly productivity from mentoring, some form of compensation will be necessary for continued faculty enthusiasm for this work. While the increased emphasis on UR and other HIPs has spurred some campuses to move to innovative approaches to delineating faculty workload (Osborn & Paul, 2010; Paul, 2012), most campuses, including COPLAC schools, still formulate workload using the standard course-based approaches. As a result, incorporating UR into the curriculum will be vital to its expansion.

Having students complete UR during the summer on a noncredit (with no tuition or fees) basis reduces any concern with fitting it into the required curriculum, but, with no tuition revenue, funding to compensate faculty must be obtained from other sources. In addition to faculty pay, there is a need for funds for student stipends. COPLAC institutions have varying percentages of Pell-eligible students, from as low as 23% to almost 60%, although most are in the 35–45% range. Participating in an unpaid summer UR experience would be difficult for many of these students who are likely to need some income from the summer to pay for tuition and other college expenses. Paying tuition for a credit-generating experience would be even more difficult. Even if year-round Pell grants are restored, obtaining external funds to provide student stipends as well as to compensate faculty will be a challenge and a reason this approach will not support a broad UR program on many campuses.

Moving Undergraduate Research From the Margins to the Center of Faculty Life

Evans (2010) captures the ironic plight of today's small public liberal arts colleges, the very site where UR should flourish:

> Ironically, small colleges are ideally positioned to develop distinguished undergraduate research programs, as they have been built on the principle of close student–faculty relationships that are foundational to helping undergraduates succeed as scholars. At the same time, though, small-college faculty are often faced with high teaching loads, broad curricular responsibilities, significant service demands, and the panoply of activities that bear a vague but real relationship with professional success in the small-college setting. (p. 31)

The University of Wisconsin-Superior, a COPLAC member institution and also a member of the University of Wisconsin (UW) System, is a prime example. A comprehensive campus of just 2,600 students, it provides undergraduate programs in 35 academic disciplines through 12 departments. Approximately half of our students are considered low-income, first-generation college students, while 68% of undergraduates work off campus.

In 1998, the UW Board of Regents designated UW-Superior as "Wisconsin's Public Liberal Arts College" as part of a UW-Superior new strategic plan to raise its profile and enhance its unique qualities. UW-Superior also serves a regional mission as the only campus in the northwest corner of the state, and, due to its location at the western reaches of Lake Superior, it has developed four research institutes focused on invasive species testing, estuarine protection, applied transportation and logistics, and maritime

NEW DIRECTIONS FOR HIGHER EDUCATION • DOI: 10.1002/he

research. Having these four institutes as campus partners has provided opportunities for UR, but it has usually been at the margins of campus life. For the past decade, UW-Superior has been a case study in the work of building UR buy-in on a small liberal arts campus.

As part of its refocusing as a liberal arts campus, UW-Superior's faculty planned (2004–2006) and initiated (2007–2009) five HIPs: Academic Service-Learning (AS-L), First Year Experience (FYE) with a First Year Seminar (FYS), Global Awareness and Education (GAE), Senior Year Experience (SYE), and Writing Across the Curriculum (WAC). These programs were developed in concert with the new Center for Excellence in Teaching and Learning (CETL). The center was established, in part, to provide professional development in best practices in teaching and learning in support of these HIPs.

The past ten years have been transformative for the campus. Four forces have been at work: the infusion of the five HIPs, the work of CETL in professional development, the requirement that the campus assess student learning outcomes, and a turnover in approximately 50% of our faculty. A timely combination of Higher Learning Commission reviews, new faculty hires, and small grants have helped to build a new culture on campus for engaging students in active learning (Cuzzo, Griffith, & Fujieda, 2014). All four of these developments set the stage for URSCA, the Undergraduate Research, Scholarship and Creative Activity Center.

In 2011, UW-Superior joined with other COPLAC campuses at the CUR workshop and decided to add UR, scholarship, and creative activity to other ways of engaging our students as a sixth HIP. An URSCA Committee was formed, composed of newer faculty who were enthusiastic about mentoring students in research and scholarship. Additional "Friends of URSCA" came from the campus research institutes. The Faculty Senate readily gave its blessing to a broad definition of URSCA that was inclusive of all disciplines, and URSCA was set to develop its goals: to build awareness, sponsor activities, engage the campus, and identify funding. The connection with the CUR workshops—through both COPLAC and the UW System—served as both catalyst and supporter to the new program. UW-Superior was in the unique position of being able to attend working sessions offered by both, which provided more opportunities for learning, planning, and assessing.

One of the first steps of the URSCA Committee was to survey the campus faculty and staff regarding their level of involvement in URSCA activities. The responses from faculty representing each academic department and research institute are summarized in Table 5.4.

Not surprisingly, barriers to more engagement in these activities were identified as "time" and "money." Many respondents also stated that UR was not recognized in their department's annual reviews or, if it was, it was considered as part of teaching load. There was a high degree of interest in strengthening URSCA activities and in developing mechanisms for formal recognition of the time and labor involved in mentoring. When compared

Table 5.4. 2011 Survey of UW Superior Faculty/Staff

Level of Involvement in URSCA Activities	Response Rate
Survey to 174 faculty and instructional staff	52% (90)
URSCA related activities in curriculum	84%
URSCA in regularly scheduled classes	76%
Actively promote URSCA in their program	82%
As part of written work	51%
Literature review	46%
Work in lab with students	36%
Monitoring student lab work	24%
Monitoring student fieldwork	41%
Mentoring UR in the last year	80%
Spending six or more hours/week mentoring	26%
Mentoring during the summer	20%

to faculty/staff involvement in the other HIPs, the level of URSCA engagement appears equal to AS-L and FYS and greater than GAE and WAC. Since the survey had not separated URSCA from Senior Capstone requirements, a second survey was administered a year later to probe this area and discover which courses included URSCA activities. When that separation occurred, 10 of 12 departments were clearly engaging in URSCA but almost exclusively in the 300- and 400-level courses in their majors and often in electives. Eight of the 10 departments actively supported students presenting at conferences, and half of these did so annually. While two department chairs stated that mentoring student research was considered in tenure and promotion reviews, it was clear that most departments did so on a case-by-case basis.

Research activities sponsored by UW-Superior include the UW System Posters in the Rotunda (http://www.wisconsin.edu/posters/), begun in 2003, and student presentations at the UW System Symposium (https://ugradsymposium.wisc.edu/) held annually around the state. A campus day of URSCA celebration was inaugurated in the spring of 2012 to showcase top student research and scholarly creative activities from all departments. This event has grown (by 50% each year, especially in the non-STEM areas) as more academic programs recognize the value of URSCA to their students. The biggest visibility for URSCA has come from cosponsoring a UW-Superior Foundation program, Summer Undergraduate Research Fellowships (SURF), which has provided students and faculty summer stipends to engage in mentored research. The year 2014 is the third year of SURF, and support for the program has enthusiastically grown from the initial commitment of $30,000 to $50,000, providing for 10 URSCA projects.

In 2013, the campus received a three-year Growth Agenda for Wisconsin Grant designed to support the development and sustainability of URSCA on campus. (No doubt support for this proposal was related to UW System's involvement in the CUR Systems Project.) The grant allowed UW-Superior to appoint an URSCA director and project assistant, establish a center dedicated to URSCA, and begin building capacity on campus in partnership with the research institutes and in the wider community. In June 2014, a daylong URSCA workshop for faculty and staff was held with the goal of incorporating URSCA activities into 100- and 200-level courses to scaffold and infuse more URSCA skills earlier in the curriculum. Changes to the 300- and 400-level courses will be possible since more students will be prepared to collaborate on URSCA. Workshops, stipends, and development mini-grants will continue into 2016.

It is too early to draw any conclusions about the long-term efficacy of the Growth Agenda grant. Yet, with the changes over the past decade, URSCA has been able to make significant progress as faculty members are eager to find ways to mentor students in their research or to have students' assistance with their own research projects. CETL has taken the lead on professional development by organizing January and June workshops. The other five HIPs are consulting and working out partnerships so that URSCA skill developments are part of other programs. If UW-Superior had not been involved in the CUR Systems Grant, URSCA, our sixth HIP, would most likely not have developed. As a catalyst it gave UW-Superior the impetus to explore its potential and to see that many on campus were engaged or interested in URSCA. As indicated earlier, it is already on par with AS-L and FYS with broad faculty and student engagement and administrative support.

In summary, the last decade has seen a significant transformation on this campus, one that has made UW-Superior a dynamic public liberal arts institution committed to engaging students in meaningful learning. The new strategic plan (Superior Visions 2020: http://www.uwsuper.edu/strategic-plan/index.cfm) specifically works URSCA into the timeline for further inclusion in the curriculum, faculty review, and funding.

Conclusions

If the expansion of high-quality UR is truly to become a COPLAC distinction, especially in an era of declining state support for public postsecondary education, then each campus must explore models of instruction that best incorporate research across the curriculum. As the UW-Superior case illustrates, the work of transformation can extend over a number of years, but the success of one campus can facilitate the work of faculty and their administrative colleagues on campuses across the consortium.

References

Cuzzo, M. S. W., Griffith, S. C., & Fujieda, E. (2014, April). *Building a culture of liberal education through collaborative professional development.* Paper presented at the Annual Higher Learning Commission Conference, Chicago, IL.

Evans, D. R. (2010). The challenge of undergraduate research. *Peer Review, 12*(2), 31.

Gates, A. Q., Teller, P. J., Bernat, A., Delgado, N., & Della-Piana, C. K. (1999). Expanding participation in undergraduate research using the Affinity Group model. *Journal of Engineering Education, 88*(4), 409–414.

Hakim, T. M. (2000). *How to develop and administer institutional undergraduate research programs.* Washington, DC: Council on Undergraduate Research.

Kierniesky, N. C. (2005). Undergraduate research in small psychology departments: Two decades later. *Teaching of Psychology, 32*(2), 84–90.

Malachowski, M., Ambos, E., Karukstis, K., & Osborn, J. (2010). *Collaborative research: Transformational learning through undergraduate research: Comprehensive support for faculty, institutions, state systems and consortia* (NSF-DUE #0920275, #0920286).

Merkel, C. A. (2001). *Undergraduate research at six research universities.* Retrieved from https://www.aau.edu/WorkArea/DownloadAsset.aspx?id=1900

Osborn, J., & Paul, E. (2010, November 11). *Moving from the periphery to the center: Faculty roles in undergraduate research.* AAC&U Network Conference on Undergraduate Research In and Across Disciplines. Retrieved from http://archive.aacu.org/pkal/documents/FacultyRolesinUndergraduateResearchPowerpoint.Durham.pdf

Paul, E. L. (2012). New directions for faculty workload models: Focusing on high-impact learning practices. In N. Hensel & E. L. Paul (Eds.), *Faculty support and undergraduate research: Innovations in faculty role definition, workload, and reward* (pp. 133–145). Washington, DC: Council of Undergraduate Research.

Pukkila, P., DeCosmo, J., Swick, D. C., & Arnold, M. S. (2007). How to engage in collaborative curriculum design to foster undergraduate inquiry and research in all disciplines. In K. K. Karukstis & T. E. Elgren (Eds.), *Developing and sustaining a research-supportive curriculum: A compendium of successful practices* (pp. 341–357). Washington, DC: Council of Undergraduate Research.

Reinen, L., Grasfils, E., Gaines, R., & Hazlett, R. (2007). Integrating research into a small geology department's curriculum. In K. K. Karukstis & T. E. Elgren (Eds.), *Developing and sustaining a research-supportive curriculum: A compendium of successful practices* (pp. 331–339). Washington, DC: Council on Undergraduate Research.

Rueckert, L. (2007). Flexible curricular structures to provide time for research within the classroom. In K. K. Karukstis & T. E. Elgren (Eds.), *Developing and sustaining a research-supportive curriculum: A compendium of successful practices* (pp. 285–294). Washington, DC: Council on Undergraduate Research.

Temple, L., Sibley, T., & Orr, A. J. (2010). *How to mentor undergraduate research.* Washington, DC: Council on Undergraduate Research.

RHONA FREE is the provost and vice president for academic affairs and professor of economics at Eastern Connecticut State University.

SUZANNE GRIFFITH is the associate dean of academic affairs, chair of the Department of Educational Leadership, and professor of educational psychology at the University of Wisconsin–Superior.

BILL SPELLMAN is the director of the Council of Public Liberal Arts Colleges and professor of history at the University of North Carolina – Asheville.

6

This chapter describes undergraduate research expansion in the Pennsylvania State System of Higher Education (PASSHE) in the context of both fiscal and student enrollment challenges.

Making Undergraduate Research a Central Strategy in High-Impact Practice Reform: The PASSHE Journey

James D. Moran III, Marilyn J. Wells, Angela Smith-Aumen

The PASSHE Context

The Pennsylvania State System of Higher Education (PASSHE) is a significant provider of higher education in the Commonwealth of Pennsylvania, with more than 112,000 degree-seeking students. The system comprises 14 universities (Bloomsburg, California, Cheyney, Clarion, East Stroudsburg, Edinboro, Indiana, Kutztown, Lock Haven, Mansfield, Millersville, Shippensburg, Slippery Rock, and West Chester Universities of Pennsylvania), four branch campuses, and numerous off-campus centers and instructional sites.

Most of the four-year institutions are master's comprehensive universities with the exception of Indiana University, which is authorized to offer PhD programs. Cheyney University is unique with its status as a Historically Black College and University. Thus, PASSHE is one of the more homogeneous systems in the country regarding Carnegie institutional classification. Nearly 90% of the PASSHE students are undergraduates and 88% are from Pennsylvania, with approximately 85% of graduates staying in the Commonwealth.

The Office of the Chancellor supports the board and the universities in carrying out the mission of the system to provide quality education at an "affordable" cost to students and families. PASSHE is considered a state agency and, as a result, the 14 universities must conform to state-level guidelines as well as board policies. Currently, the state provides approximately 27% of PASSHE's funding, with the remainder coming from students and their families.

Undergraduate Research in the PASSHE Context. As many of PASSHE's faculty members have pointed out, undergraduate research

NEW DIRECTIONS FOR HIGHER EDUCATION, no. 169, Spring 2015 © 2015 Wiley Periodicals, Inc.
Published online in Wiley Online Library (wileyonlinelibrary.com) • DOI: 10.1002/he.20123

advocacy is not a new concept, and we should interpret it broadly, to encompass scholarship and creative activities. However, clearly the attention to undergraduate research, especially at the system level, has increased over the past decade. Thus, perhaps the major question is not *Why undergraduate research?* Rather, the key questions might be *Why undergraduate research now?* and *What has changed in the context of higher education?*

The past decade has seen a major shift in the demands on higher education. We see three drivers for the increased attention to providing quality student experiences, including undergraduate research.

Driver 1: Postsecondary attainment. States and system offices are now keenly aware of the linkages between postsecondary attainment and economic vitality. Although targets and the route to the solutions may differ, this perception appears to cut across party lines and is generally supported by the National Governors Association (2013a).

The goal remains the same whether looking at President Obama's initiative for increased postsecondary success, efforts of the Lumina Foundation (2014), Complete College America's (2013) focus, or that of the United States Chamber of Commerce (2012).

Driver 2: Declining state funding and enrollments. At the same time as we have seen an increase in the external demands for colleges and universities to perform, we have also seen a decline in state funding, especially in Pennsylvania. Across the country, a change has also occurred in the way funds are distributed to higher education, with increased emphasis on performance and outcomes. As of March 2014, 25 of the 50 states have adopted some form of performance-based funding for higher education (Hurley, Harnish, & Parker, 2014).

With the decline in state funding, public universities in Pennsylvania have become more dependent upon revenue from tuition and fees for base operations (Figure 6.1). The dilemma is that many universities in PASSHE have real limits on increasing the total cost of attendance due to relatively high numbers of lower income (Pell-eligible) students. A recent analysis completed for PASSHE indicated that for at least one third of PASSHE institutions, an increase in total cost of attendance by $1,000 could actually result in less total revenue due to a significant decline in the number of potential students able to afford such an increase.

Coupled with a decline in state revenues, Pennsylvania has also seen a significant decline in high school graduates. This decline varies geographically and is especially prominent in northern and western Pennsylvania. The percentage of high school students moving on to college has fallen from 72% in 2004–2005 to 67% in 2012–2013 (Pennsylvania Department of Education, 2014). Even more dramatic are the population shifts from 1960 to 2013 in cities such as Harrisburg (down 38%); Pittsburg (down 49%); Erie (down 27%); or Youngstown, Ohio (down 61%).

Here again, the relationship between student retention, graduation rates, and engagement in high-impact practices (Kuh, 2008) is critical.

NEW DIRECTIONS FOR HIGHER EDUCATION • DOI: 10.1002/he

**Figure 6.1. PASSHE E&G Appropriation Versus Tuition and Fees[a]
From 1983/1984 to 2011/2012**

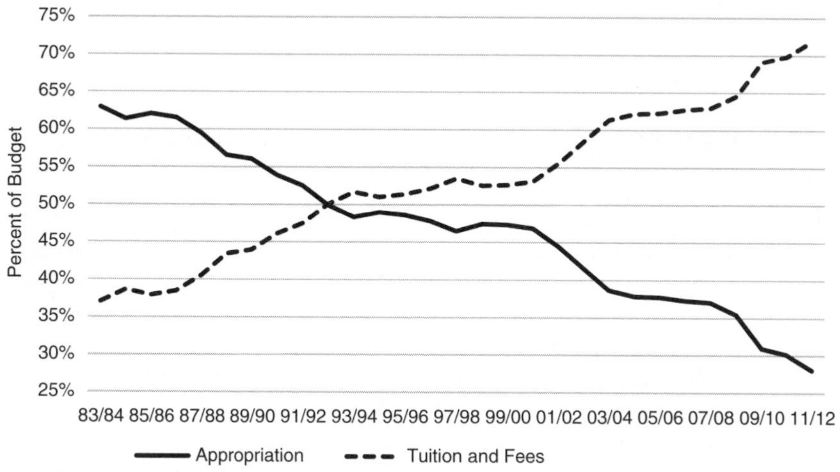

[a]Includes all other miscellaneous revenue sources.

With the triple challenge of fewer students, decline in state funding, and limits on institutional capacity to raise tuition/fees, attention to retention becomes a necessity and the primary avenue to drive both student success and fiscal stability. Retention is now thought to be an easier route to increase net revenue than is recruitment (Jones, 2013). Programs that support high-impact practices, such as undergraduate research, should be viewed as investments that provide a rate of return through the retention of students. In PASSHE, we utilized that strategy through the use of the Equity Scorecard™ (Bensimon, Dowd, & Hanson, 2013; Bensimon, Dowd, Witham, Lyman, & Moran, 2014; Bensimon & Malcom, 2012) to track the success of underrepresented and low-income students. With an average cost of attendance of $18,500 per year, we recognized that an annual investment of nearly $500,000 dollars would pay for itself through the retention of just 28 students annually across all institutions—an average of two students per university.

Driver 3: Academic preparation. The third driver is the perception that higher education is not preparing students for the workforce. In *Academically Adrift*, Arum and Roksa (2011) questioned whether college added value to students' critical thinking abilities, a core skill sought by employers.

Clearly, undergraduate research is a pivotal strategy to enable desirable workforce attributes such as innovation, critical thinking, teamwork, and oral and written communication. With the U.S. economy demanding a more educated workforce, states are looking to higher education to more effectively and efficiently meet this demand. The National Governors

Association report *Beyond Completion Enabling Governors to Evaluate the Outcomes of Postsecondary Education* (NGA, 2013b) advocates for a comprehensive approach to address the shift from simply measuring inputs to a broader emphasis on outcomes and defining the relationship between resources and results.

Relating PASSHE to the Higher Education System Context for Student Success

It is not unusual for a state's goals to be aligned with, and integral to, the goals of state system offices. Moreover, public systems of higher education must respond to their state's changing demographics to provide not just equity of opportunity but also equity of success for the state's populace. To meet the state and national needs for increased credentials, national-level data (Engle, Yeado, Brusi, & Cruz, 2012) indicate that more of the same will not work; we need to change the slope of change.

The metrics of success at the system and state levels have changed partly because the demographics of public institutions have changed. The shift has been from *exclusion and inputs* (how many students did we deny admission) to *inclusion and outputs* (how many students did we graduate, and how many of those we graduated were part of the newly emerging workforce: lower income, underrepresented, and returning adults).

The key questions are then "What works?"; "How do we scale up those experiences so that opportunities are equitable regardless of student characteristics such as race, heritage, or income?"; and "Why is it critical for a system to promote undergraduate research?"

Undergraduate Research as a Signature Strategy for Student Success in PASSHE

At PASSHE, we recognized that we would not be able to adequately address increasing completion rates without attending to issues of demography and equity. As PASSHE embarked on work with the Council on Undergraduate Research (CUR; Malachowski, Ambos, Karukstis, & Osborn, 2010) and other organizations, the changing state context described earlier confronted us.

Nonetheless, the faculty and administrators on the university CUR teams maintained their commitment and enthusiasm as the project progressed. This engagement was augmented by other initiatives occurring simultaneously across PASSHE. All 14 universities were engaged in *The Equity Scorecard*™ through PASSHE's partnership with the Center for Urban Education housed at the University of Southern California. Similarly, selected universities were engaged in the U.S. Education Delivery Institute's *Access to Success Initiative* (a project of the National Association of System Heads and The Education Trust) and PASSHE's *Professional Science*

NEW DIRECTIONS FOR HIGHER EDUCATION • DOI: 10.1002/he

Master's Initiative (supported by The Alfred P. Sloan Foundation). Each of these involved campus teams of faculty working together to close achievement gaps and improve student success. Therefore, we had four major system-wide, university-based, and collaborative initiatives all centered on a team approach, and several faculty served on more than one team, broadening and deepening connections, essential to the success of the CUR project.

As a result, undergraduate research, along with these other initiatives, became recognized not only as an academic opportunity but also as a central retention strategy. PASSHE finance officers have now begun to view undergraduate research as an investment, rather than as an additional or tangential expense, for enrollment management and future revenues.

Performance Funding.   At the same time when PASSHE was involved in the CUR project, our Board of Governors was embarking on a system-wide strategic plan and revising PASSHE's performance funding model (PASSHE, 2014). Universities were provided the opportunity to (a) identify five "optional measures" that could be distinct from university to university and (b) design "custom measures" that would be unique to the institution, based on their university goals. This latter opportunity was the opening for several universities to specify high-impact practices, especially undergraduate research, as pertinent to student success.

Additionally, based on analysis of data, PASSHE eliminated the optional measure of "instructional productivity" (i.e., student credit hours per faculty member) in the performance funding model; increases in the measure were largely driven by external economic conditions. Institutions were asked to replace instructional productivity with a measure of the quality of the student experience, which provided yet another opportunity for institutions to add measures related to undergraduate research. Without PASSHE's involvement in the CUR project, attention to these alternate measures may not have been so readily formalized.

The Initial Impetus for Pursuing Undergraduate Research. PASSHE's specific attention to increasing opportunities for undergraduate research was based on data conversations with other system officers and several related system-wide efforts: (a) increasing the opportunities for students, especially low-income and underrepresented minorities, to participate in distinctive educational experiences; and (b) increasing student success and graduation rates (performance funding metric), as well as student retention (i.e., tuition revenue; Finley & McNair, 2013).

The First Steps for the PASSHE-CUR Project.   By using a coordinated effort focused on undergraduate research, each PASSHE university was able to assess where they were with regard to undergraduate research and also where they wanted to be. This process differed at each of the 14 universities, but shared stories enabled all to move forward within a reasonable time period. Several universities quickly realized that institutionalizing undergraduate research is connected to a broader effort of enhancing student success via high-impact practices, viewing the task as one that required cultural change on the campuses.

As a consequence, many universities undertook an initial assessment of current activity and available resources. The importance of leveraging the expertise of selected faculty and identifying "champions" on campus emerged as an initial tactic.

Curriculum Revision and Reenvisioning.   Enhancement of undergraduate research experiences across PASSHE coincided with discussions of general education efforts at several universities. This coordinated effort proved advantageous because several universities were reframing their general education models. The "distribution" model was giving way to the adoption of the Association of American Colleges and Universities (AAC&U, 2013) *Liberal Education and America's Promise* (LEAP) model.

At some universities, the reconsideration of general education was driven by upcoming regional accreditation visits by the Middle States Commission on Higher Education (2011). The drive by higher education accrediting bodies for well-articulated learning outcomes has been evidence of a fundamental shift in educational philosophy and instructional modes.

Furthermore, we recognize that there is mounting evidence that academic rigor (defined as access to learning activities, such as high-impact practices) increases the odds that students will graduate. Faculty members exposed to this logical sequence are now more comfortable with the "completion agenda" because quality is not distinct from increased degree production. Deep involvement of the faculty is critical to increasing student success, retention rates, and graduation rates through their mentoring role in high-impact practices such as undergraduate research experiences.

Inventorying Undergraduate Research in PASSHE: Insights and Challenges.   As each university formalized efforts, what often emerged was a comprehensive inventory/self-assessment of their undergraduate research experiences. Many were surprised at the extent of existing opportunities for students, but most had not compiled their activities into a comprehensive system. Overall, we learned that there was more going on in PASSHE than many expected, but it was not necessarily visible nor were institutional definitions consistent. Adoption of a broad definition of undergraduate scholarship was needed in order to move beyond STEM disciplines. The system-wide attention to undergraduate research led to alliances being formed across campuses.

Several challenges also surfaced in the self-assessment including (a) "what counts" as undergraduate research? and (b) how does one capture or measure both the nature of the experiences and the number of students participating? University-level data were often not available for tracking success, and disaggregated data to assess equity were not available. This led to identifying a common measure of undergraduate research efforts and increased visibility of these efforts through the inclusion of undergraduate research as a performance indicator for several universities.

NEW DIRECTIONS FOR HIGHER EDUCATION • DOI: 10.1002/he

We were also seeking creative solutions for incorporating research experiences into the curriculum, such that opportunities are presented to a wider range of students, especially underrepresented and low-income students. Fundamentally, the question is how to effectively scale up (what may be) individual opportunities across the campus. Such curricular revisions are not easy because we cannot simply "add on" to the existing program given the drive to reduce time-to-graduation and thus the cost to the student. Several universities also recognized the dilemma of serving the various types of students: how do we find equivalent experiences for residential students, for online students, for working adults, and for transfers? For assessment, universities need to "tag" courses and independent study experiences as "research-intensive," track enrollments, and monitor the nature of the experience to "earn" the label of research-intensive parallel to what is frequently done for "writing-intensive" courses.

Practical issues also emerged from university assessments. Some laboratories were primarily designed, scheduled, and staffed purely for instruction. In addition, the faculty teaching/mentoring associated with vibrant undergraduate research may not be formally recognized by the university in any form of evaluation for merit, tenure, or promotion.

PASSHE's Actions to Sustain and Enhance Undergraduate Research. At this point, whether we have been successful in developing a sustainable culture of high-impact practices and undergraduate research across PASSHE is still unknown. Nonetheless, the preliminary work of the institutional faculties has identified many promising actions and recommendations.

The positive link between undergraduate research and student retention, and the imperative within PASSHE to retain more students clearly indicates that we need to provide students with earlier research experiences. Several institutions suggested incorporating components of research in first-year experience courses. One institution implemented a first-year "Research and Mentoring" course; another has developed a four-year scaffolding plan to infuse undergraduate research into its curriculum.

Many faculty members proposed ideas for additional funding to help support the undergraduate research expansion effort. Since the CUR workshops, several institutions implemented/planned summer undergraduate research grants under faculty mentorship. Within PASSHE, developing a stronger grant-seeking culture could also help provide more funding for student research. One institution has allocated a portion of all indirect revenues from sponsored research for this purpose; another did this on a grant-by-grant basis. Reallocating work-study funds was another strategy proposed, as was approaching student government and redirecting some student activity monies to help support this effort by students, especially for travel funds for student presentations.

Changing the culture also includes recognizing the value of student mentoring by faculty colleagues and administrators in the promotion and

NEW DIRECTIONS FOR HIGHER EDUCATION • DOI: 10.1002/he

tenure process. One institution was successful in including undergraduate mentoring in its evaluation criteria of "service." Visibility of the activities via campus-level awards and formal research days is also important. Upon completion of the CUR workshops, we held the first system-wide Undergraduate STEM Research Conference, with participation by 12 of the 14 universities.

Coordinating activities across departments can also create more opportunities for students. Several institutions have now created "centers" and provide part-time faculty directors.

Participating in the CUR workshop program opened the eyes of many to the level of activity that was occurring on their campus. One university identified a 400% increase in *reported* undergraduate research over two years, an increase that was due solely to educating the faculty about the broad nature of undergraduate research, scholarship, and creative activity. Through its efforts, this campus has created a culture of undergraduate research that will be clearly sustainable.

Activities of the PASSHE System Office to Support Undergraduate Research.   The system office has recognized that we could provide support for university efforts by taking the lead in some cases and simply providing the flexibility for change in others. The Office of the Chancellor led the effort in developing communication channels to promote the importance of undergraduate research and how it is connected to other initiatives, such as the completion agenda and equity.

Regular meetings with the chief academic officers for the 14 PASSHE universities would often touch on these issues and how undergraduate research could be incorporated into performance funding and strategic plans. Presentations about high-impact practices were provided to the meeting of the University Council of Trustees and the System Board of Governors. One of the critical messages is that undergraduate research is linked to equity, to workforce needs, to the drive for STEM degrees, and to program quality (Lingenfelter & Moran, 2011; Moran & Bliley, 2012; Wells & Moran, 2013).

System-level efforts included specifying the criteria for additional faculty professional development funds for innovative teaching/learning practices to include undergraduate research. System representatives incorporated comments about undergraduate research, and other high-impact practices, into departmental chair professional development efforts. In addition, at PASSHE's High-Impact Practices Conference held at Clarion University, directed discussions were held with various universities on how to measure undergraduate research and how to advocate for inclusion of high-impact practices into their strategic plans or performance funding model.

Policies have been developed that recognize student involvement in technology transfer and enable students to more readily share courses and student experiences across all universities. Funding has been provided to support university-led, system-wide conferences on Innovation in

Teaching, on High-Impact Practices, and specifically Undergraduate Research. Sponsorship has been obtained for undergraduate business competitions and a day at the state capital that highlights undergraduate research. Faculties have banded together to sponsor and publish a system-wide undergraduate research journal to create an outlet for student pride and visibility for their efforts.

PASSHE is planning to further apply and integrate the lessons learned from working with CUR. In particular, PASSHE is leveraging this in our work with Access to Success, U.S. Education Delivery Institute, and the Center for Urban Education, all within the context of undergraduate research. We have learned to (a) look at our disaggregated student access and success data, (b) use the process of inquiry to address the opportunities and barriers, (c) develop a specific plan to move forward involving the key players, and (d) develop routines to monitor our progress.

The System Office's Vision for the Future.   Throughout PASSHE's engagement in the CUR initiative, and in this volume, the role of the system office has been discussed. Involvement by a system is not an essential component for the promotion of high-impact practices and undergraduate research, but we have learned that PASSHE institutions and faculty members have found it helpful. One consistent theme has been the value that faculty members have placed on cross-institutional support for each other and the coordination for those conversations provided by the system office. The ability to share strategies (both successes and frustrations) helped keep many on track. Involvement by the system office also provided individual faculty members with a sense that they were part of something larger than their own program and connected them with like-minded colleagues. The system office also played a key role in providing strategies to track data to monitor success.

We now recognize that undergraduate research is not just an academic issue. One institution suggested that their proposed Undergraduate Research Council includes members from the enrollment management division and the faculty professional development committee. Scaling up high-impact practices is an investment in the future of the institution and an investment in the social, economic, and cultural vitality of the state.

Moving Forward

The effort to place high-impact practices, including undergraduate research, front and center as part of PASSHE's completion agenda is reflected in the new strategic plan reviewed by the Board of Governors in January 2014.

By institutionalizing undergraduate research, PASSHE aims to enhance the way that students learn, faculty members teach, and courses are delivered to optimize student success. The impetus provided by participating in the CUR project enhanced the integrity and quality of academic programs, and provided an opportunity to increase the success of undergraduate students through engagement in research experiences. We believe that undergraduate research is at the intersection of the interests of students, faculty, the universities, and the system (Osborn & Karukstis, 2009).

References

Arum, R., & Roksa, J. (2011). *Academically adrift: Limited learning on college campuses.* Chicago, IL: University of Chicago Press.

Association of American Colleges and Universities (AAC&U). (2013). *Liberal education and America's promise.* Washington, DC. Retrieved from http://www.aacu.org/leap/index.cfm

Bensimon, E., Dowd, A., & Hanson, D. (2013). Assessing equity in high-impact practices toolkit. In A. Finley & T. McNair (Eds.), *Assessing underserved students' engagement in high-impact practices* (pp. 35–47). Washington, DC: Association of American Colleges and Universities.

Bensimon, E., Dowd, A., Witham, K., Lyman, B., & Moran, J. (2014, April). *The power of action research for innovation in accountability practice and policy.* Presented at the Annual Meeting of the American Education Research Association, Philadelphia, PA.

Bensimon, E., & Malcom, L. (2012). *Confronting equity issues on campus: Implementing the equity scorecard.* Sterling, VA: Stylus.

Complete College America. (2013). *The game changers: Complete College America, Indianapolis.* Retrieved from http://completecollege.org/pdfs/CCA%20Nat%20Report%20Oct18-FINAL-singles.pdf

Engle, J., Yeado, J., Brusi, R., & Cruz, J. (2012). *Replenishing opportunity in America: The 2012 midterm report of public higher education systems in the access to success initiative.* Washington, DC: The Education Trust.

Finley, A., & McNair, T. (2013). *Assessing underserved students' engagement in high-impact practices.* Washington, DC: Association of American Colleges and Universities.

Hurley, D., Harnish, T., & Parker, E. (2014). *State outlook: Fiscal and state policy issues affecting postsecondary education.* Washington, DC: American Association of State Colleges and Universities. Retrieved from http://www.aascu.org/policy/publications/aascu-special-reports/stateoutlookjuly2014.pdf

Jones, D. (2013, October). *Comments made at the Complete College America 2013 Annual Convening.* Salt Lake City, UT: Complete College America.

Kuh, G. D. (2008). *High-impact practices: What they are, who has access to them, and why they matter.* Washington DC: Association of American Colleges and Universities.

Lingenfelter, M., & Moran, J. (2011, April). *Board strategies for college completion.* Los Angeles, CA: Association of Governing Boards (AGB) National Conference on Trusteeship.

Lumina Foundation. (2014). *A stronger nation through higher education.* Indianapolis, IN: Lumina Foundation. Retrieved from http://www.luminafoundation.org/resources/a-stronger-nation-through-higher-education

Malachowski, M., Ambos, E., Karukstis, K., & Osborn, J. (2010). *Collaborative research: Transformational learning through undergraduate research: Comprehensive support for faculty, institutions, state systems and consortia* (NSF-DUE #0920275, #0920286).

Middle States Commission on Higher Education. (2011). *Characteristics of excellence in higher education: Requirements of affiliation and standards for accreditation.* Philadelphia, PA: Author.

Moran, J., & Bliley, S. (2012, December). *Transitioning to evidenced-based planning as the foundation for resource allocation.* Paper presented at the annual meeting of the Middle States Commission on Higher Education, Philadelphia, PA.

National Governors Association (NGA). (2013a). *America works: Education and training for tomorrow's jobs—The benefit of a more education workforce to individuals and the economy.* Retrieved from http://www.nga.org/files/live/sites/NGA/files/pdf/2014/1402-Moodys-AmericaWorks_35f.pdf

National Governors Association (NGA). (2013b). *Beyond completion: Enabling governors to evaluate the outcomes of postsecondary education.* Retrieved from http://www.nga.org/files/live/sites/NGA/files/pdf/2013/1309BeyondCompletionPaper.pdf

Osborn, J. M., & Karukstis, K. K. (2009). The benefits of undergraduate research, scholarship, and creative activity. In M. Boyd & J. Wesemann (Eds.), *Broadening participation in undergraduate research: Fostering excellence and enhancing the impact* (pp. 41–53). Washington, DC: Council on Undergraduate Research.

PASSHE. (2014). *Strategic Plan 2020: Rising to the challenge.* Harrisburg, PA. Retrieved from http://www.passhe.edu/inside/bog/Documents/Strategic%20Plan%202020%20Rising%20to%20the%20Challenge_dh.pdf

Pennsylvania Department of Education. (2014). *Graduate data and statistics.* Retrieved from http://www.education.state.pa.us/portal/server.pt/community/graduates/7426

United States Chamber of Commerce. (2012). *Leaders & laggards: A state-by-state report card on public postsecondary education.* Washington, DC. Retrieved from http://education.uschamber.com/reportcard/

Wells, M., & Moran, J. (2013, May). *Creating a pathway for institutional success.* National Conference for Race and Ethnicity in American Higher Education, New Orleans, LA.

JAMES D. MORAN III is the former vice chancellor for academic and student affairs at PASSHE. He currently serves as the provost and vice president for Academic Affairs at the University of South Dakota.

MARILYN J. WELLS is the former vice provost and graduate dean at East Stroudsburg University. She currently serves as the provost and senior vice president for Academic Affairs at Minnesota State University, Mankato

ANGELA SMITH-AUMEN is the director of sponsored programs at PASSHE.

7

Securing funding for undergraduate research activities is critical to a vibrant program. Strategies for obtaining funding are described in this chapter.

Fostering Resources for Undergraduate Research at the City University of New York

Effie S. MacLachlan, Avrom J. Caplan

Introduction

The City University of New York (CUNY) is the largest public urban university system in the United States; in 2012 nearly 240,000 undergraduate students were enrolled in the 11 four-year and seven community colleges that span the five boroughs of New York City. The CUNY student body is a reflection of the ethnically and culturally diverse demographics of the city: African-American and Hispanic undergraduates each comprise more than a quarter of the student body (26% and 29%, respectively), and Asians comprise nearly 20%. In addition, 40% of undergraduates were born outside of the United States, and 45% are the first generation in their family to attend college.

Engaging students in undergraduate research (UR) is a high-impact practice that increases student retention, graduation rates, and overall academic success (Brownell & Swaner, 2010; Eagan et al., 2013; Graham, Frederick, Byars-Winston, Hunter, & Handelsman, 2013; Lopatto, 2004; Russell, Hancock, & McCullough, 2007). UR programming has been shown to be particularly effective in attracting and retaining underrepresented groups in STEM disciplines (Summers & Hrabowski, 2006). Mentored research experiences also contribute to effective career preparation and promote an innovation-oriented culture.

Most CUNY colleges are principally undergraduate institutions, although The City College of New York (CCNY) and Hunter College award joint PhD degrees with the CUNY Graduate Center in certain fields. The institution as a whole, however, has a strong research culture, even among faculty at community colleges. All CUNY faculty are governed by a single union contract that does not distinguish between faculty at four-year and

NEW DIRECTIONS FOR HIGHER EDUCATION, no. 169, Spring 2015 © 2015 Wiley Periodicals, Inc.
Published online in Wiley Online Library (wileyonlinelibrary.com) • DOI: 10.1002/he.20124

community colleges when delineating the requirements for tenure and promotion. All faculty are expected to engage in scholarly activities, which can include research, to maintain good standing and advance in their respective departments. It is therefore common to find professors across the colleges and across disciplines who involve students in their research endeavors.

Most undergraduates who are engaged in research at CUNY operate under a traditional apprenticeship model, working directly with a faculty member on his or her research projects. Several programmatic alternatives to this model that find creative ways to broaden participation via classroom instruction have been developed by CUNY faculty and are starting to be implemented in courses across the university.

Finding direct financial support for students is one of the main challenges when it comes to institutionalizing UR at CUNY schools. Nearly 40% of CUNY undergraduates live in households earning less than $20,000 per year, and 30% work for pay more than 20 hours per week. Stipend support for undergraduate researchers often frees them from having to make a choice between working to support themselves and working toward their education. This chapter will explore some of the programs that individual faculty members and colleges have developed and instituted to address this challenge.

Centralized Support for Research

The Vice Chancellor for Research, Gillian Small, takes overall responsibility for all research activities at the university, and under her leadership CUNY supports several initiatives aimed to serve both faculty and students.

An award created and funded by a provision in the collective bargaining agreement between the university and the faculty union—the Professional Staff Congress—provides support for professors across all disciplines. This program, which is administered by the CUNY Research Foundation, awarded over 850 one-year grants ranging from $3,500 to $12,000 in 2013.

Two university-wide programs designed to further individual faculty endeavors, the Collaborative Incentive Research Grant and the Community College Collaborative Incentive Research Grant, provide annual faculty awards ranging from $15,000 to $30,000. These awards are provided by the Office of the Vice Chancellor for Research (OVCR) and are intended to foster multidisciplinary collaborations and to seed research that will lead to applications to national funding agencies. Faculty are encouraged by the grant guidelines to include undergraduates in their research efforts.

In contrast to these more traditional investigator-focused funding models, several newer institutional efforts led by the OVCR are specifically designed to engage undergraduate students in research. These efforts are a direct result of a series of NSF-sponsored workshops organized by CUR (Malachowski, Ambos, Karukstis, & Osborn, 2010) that brought central office and campus administrators together for the first time to discuss the ways in which UR could be institutionalized at both the system and college levels. Based on the discussions at these workshops, the CUNY central office has organized a CUNY Undergraduate Research Council to coordinate efforts across the campuses and has created a UR website dedicated to sharing information and best practices from around the university.

CUNY's engagement with CUR has also influenced the creation of a new initiative designed to broaden participation by undergraduates in research by using curricular and classroom-based approaches. In the spring of 2014, the OVCR sponsored a workshop entitled *Research in the Classroom: Integrating Authentic Research Into the Undergraduate Curriculum* to generate dialogue on the topic within and across campuses. An Idea Grant award competition was launched that seeks to seed innovative approaches to integrating authentic research into the curriculum. The goal of broadening student participation by incorporating faculty research into classroom activities is a relatively new area for CUNY as a system; however, there are several federally funded models utilizing this approach being employed on individual campuses (Hoskins, Lopatto, & Stevens, 2011; Muth & McEntee, 2014).

The OVCR also supports a CUNY Summer Undergraduate Research Program (C-SURP) with additional funding from the Alfred P. Sloan Foundation. The C-SURP enables students to participate in research projects in their chosen field of science and to learn to communicate effectively with scientists across disciplines. The C-SURP augments several efforts to engage undergraduates via a variety of programs at individual colleges, from NSF-funded research experiences for undergraduates (REUs) to larger institutional grants as described next.

Commitments to Undergraduate Research at CUNY Colleges

Strategic planning efforts undertaken by each college are strong indicators of both system-wide and college-level priorities and commitments to resource allocation. Performance targets and goals are set within the framework of an overarching university master plan, which is then operationalized at the college level through the CUNY Performance Management Process (PMP). The annual PMP reports, in conjunction with more aspirational institution-specific strategic planning documents, provide a useful window into tracking institutional priorities regarding resource allocation for UR.

The CUNY PMP process establishes annual university-wide goals and performance targets for all of the CUNY colleges. The PMP is organized around three overarching goals: (a) raise academic quality, (b) improve student success, and (c) enhance financial and management effectiveness. Each college's PMP reports are in alignment with the goals and targets of the university; however, they also reflect the individual missions and circumstances of each campus.

NEW DIRECTIONS FOR HIGHER EDUCATION • DOI: 10.1002/he

Most of the colleges that address UR in their performance reports include their accomplishments and plans under the goal of improving student success. For example, in its 2013–2014 PMP report, Baruch College outlines plans to benchmark the "number of students currently engaged in independent research activities to increase that number in subsequent years." To establish these benchmarks, Baruch plans to identify the existing independent research opportunities, ascertain the number of undergraduates who engage in these opportunities, and task the Provost's Office of Undergraduate Research (OUR) with creating an honors track for students engaged in independent research.

In the New York City College of Technology's most recent PMP report, the college commits to increasing the number of undergraduates and faculty engaged in research and mentoring, respectively. The PMP report also states that "guidelines will be established for several levels of UR, funds will again be designated to support student travel to conferences, and faculty development for mentoring will continue." The York College PMP states that the "student experience will also benefit from a continued focus on faculty mentored undergraduate research." This commitment is reinforced by one of the educational initiatives at the heart of the York College Strategic Plan for 2010–2020: the expansion of "opportunities for undergraduate research and creative activities across the disciplines."

The college-specific strategic planning documents are also a good indicator of priorities in regard to resource allocation. The Brooklyn College president's foreword in the 2011–2016 Strategic Plan states that Brooklyn College recognizes "the need for increased support for high-impact learning opportunities," such as student research projects. The overview of the 2009–2013 Strategic Plan for The City College of New York (CCNY) states "the overriding purpose of City College's planning and development for the next four years is to transform CCNY into a research-oriented institution." The report notes "departments in science and engineering have a long history of sponsored undergraduate research programs that should serve as a model in other divisions."

The College of Staten Island's (CSI) 2011–2016 Strategic Plan cites the goal of expanding and supporting student research programs. CSI aims to (a) provide institutional leadership across disciplines to take advantage of external funding opportunities for student research, (b) enable the development of faculty–student mentoring relationships, (c) improve assessment of student research opportunities and achievements, and (d) enhance outreach to students regarding research opportunities. CSI also intends to expand a stipend-matching program for undergraduate researchers. The Division of Science & Technology at CSI has a program that offers summer UR fellowships to give motivated students the opportunity to become involved in the summer research activities of externally funded faculty mentors. The college and the faculty member share the cost of the student stipend.

NEW DIRECTIONS FOR HIGHER EDUCATION • DOI: 10.1002/he

Hunter College asserts, "we can state clearly what we aspire to be when we have realized the plan—a research-oriented, student-centered university," in its Strategic Plan covering Academic Years 2012–2020. The Hunter strategic planning committee anticipates that students will take an active role in realizing Hunter's vision for a research-oriented university model, and the institutionalization of Hunter's existing Undergraduate Research Initiative is just one example of this. The 2010–2014 Master Plan for John Jay College identifies research as one of the five "domains of excellence" for the college. John Jay seeks to challenge the divide between teaching and research. The college actively seeks faculty who are "teacher/scholars," "who value the participation of students, including undergraduates, in their research."

Lehman College states in its Strategic Planning Council Report for 2009–2019 that the college aims to improve its graduation rates by providing funded UR opportunities to full-time students. The vision statement in the Medgar Evers College Strategic Plan states that "faculty actively involve students in discipline-specific and interdisciplinary research and in the creative arts." The Queens College 2013–2018 Strategic Plan endorses an environment in which learning and research intersect: "students will be immersed in a thriving intellectual community of active learning, including experiential education, service learning, and faculty-led research opportunities."

The commitment to UR exhibited by the four-year CUNY schools is also evident in the PMP reports produced by CUNY community colleges. We have recently described efforts to promote UR at CUNY community colleges in detail (Caplan & MacLachlan, 2014). Several colleges, including the Borough of Manhattan Community College, Kingsborough Community College, and LaGuardia Community College, emphasize UR as a tool for student success. Indeed, Queensborough Community College has institutionalized UR by explicitly incorporating it as a high-impact practice in its relatively new advising and enrollment strategy called the Freshman Academies.

Examples of Institutionalization of Undergraduate Research at the CUNY Colleges

Obtaining resources for UR occurs through both individual and institutional efforts; in the most successful cases, these efforts synergize to generate self-sustaining programs. Several different approaches taken by CUNY colleges follow.

John Jay College of Criminal Justice: PRISM. The Program for Research Initiatives for Science Majors (PRISM) at John Jay College of Criminal Justice is one of the best examples at CUNY of a program explicitly focused on creating research opportunities for undergraduates that has led to the institutionalization of UR for the whole college.

NEW DIRECTIONS FOR HIGHER EDUCATION • DOI: 10.1002/he

In 1999, John Jay received funds from the New York State Educational Department College Science, Technology, and Engineering Program (CSTEP) to provide research training and stipends for a small cohort of students. Anthony Carpi, PRISM codirector, who was a new assistant professor in the Department of Sciences at the time, recalls how one of the primary impetuses for the nascent PRISM program was the very high attrition rate among STEM undergraduates. The CSTEP contributed to a programmatic reorientation that recognized and supported mentored UR training. The CSTEP-sponsored students not only received recognition for their research activities but they also applied and were accepted to graduate programs at a much higher rate than the general population.

According to Carpi, Ronan, Falconer, Boyd, and Lents (2013), UR gained further institutional legitimacy with the formation of PRISM in 2006. While funded from various sources, this unified program formalized and codified research activities, centralized initiatives, and provided coordination for future funding efforts (Carpi et al., 2013). The PRISM program was formed out of the amalgamation of externally funded programs, starting with the CSTEP, and subsequently with a United States Department of Education Title V grant (awarded to John Jay as a Hispanic Serving Institution) and a Minority Science and Engineering Improvement Program (MSEIP) grant. This act of branding, merging previously disparate programs into one organizational structure and giving it a memorable name, helped promote the program among students and raised the profile of the PRISM program. PRISM branding also led to greater institutional buy-in and the opportunity to pursue new funding streams.

PRISM funds are used for student stipends, a small supply budget for faculty mentors, travel to conferences, and preparatory courses for graduate entrance exams. As increased retention and graduation rates became evident, the college administration began to allocate more internal resources to the science department in particular and UR in general. The PRISM project "catalyzed a self-perpetuating cycle of growth and expansion" (Carpi & Lents, 2013, para. 2).

Undergraduate research has been further embedded into the academic culture at John Jay by the hiring of more research-active faculty and through curricular changes. The number of full-time faculty in the science department has increased from 12 in 1999 to 26 in 2014.

The nexus between institutional and individual resource building occurs when faculty take advantage of the infrastructure that enables them to integrate undergraduates into their research projects, which in turn makes them more competitive for funding from federal agencies. Faculty gain access to resources—both monetary and human—to conduct their research in a resource-poor public institution. Undergraduate researchers are generating preliminary data that contribute to grant proposals and publications for faculty members. In 1999, only two out of 12 full-time faculty members had external funding; by 2012, this figure had risen to nine out of 22 faculty members who had secured external research grants.

The PRISM program has also demonstrated that it provides an effective model for creating successful student outcomes. Since its creation, student enrollment in UR has increased each year; PRISM students have contributed to a significant scholarly output that includes conference presentations and journal articles, and many PRISM students pursue advanced degrees. These successes did not go unnoticed by both the college and university administrations. However, enhancing UR opportunities in the sciences can be an expensive proposition in terms of research labs and facilities. In the mid-2000s, the university and the college decided to invest in research infrastructure with more funds for instrumentation, and by 2009 John Jay had built 22 new research laboratories. In 2010, the provost of John Jay College created a permanent OUR that operates in parallel to the PRISM program and serves the students not in PRISM. The hiring of a full-time PRISM coordinator in 2014 provides clear evidence of institutionalization of UR.

The road to the expansion and institutionalization of UR at John Jay was a long one that began in the late 1990s among a small group of committed science faculty, who figured out how to create a coherent UR enterprise out of a small number of publicly funded programs. As is often the case, success breeds success; when PRISM showed that it could improve retention and graduation rates in STEM as well as increase the numbers of students going onto graduate school, the college administration was further encouraged and increased promotion of UR as a high-impact practice deserving of a greater commitment of resources.

Hunter College: SciMON.   Hunter College has a history of successfully obtaining large institutional grants that provide educational and research opportunities for its students; most of these grants are targeted to serve underrepresented groups in STEM disciplines. Several externally funded programs provide students with access to UR opportunities and stipend support, including the NSF-funded Louis Stokes Alliance for Minority Participation (LSAMP), the Minority Access to Research Centers (MARC), and the Minority Biomedical Research Support–Research Initiative for Scientific Enhancement (MBRS-RISE) programs funded by the National Institutes of Health.

To create an organizational infrastructure that encompassed all of these programs, Hunter was awarded an I^3 (Innovation through Institutional Integration) grant from the NSF in 2010 (Rabinowitz, Nicols-Grinenko, Lambe, Greenbaum, & Gardner, 2010). Hunter's I^3 funded project is called SciMON (Science Mathematics Opportunities Network) and is designed to transform how students access and benefit from STEM enrichment programs at Hunter. The SciMON program aims to recruit students at an earlier stage in their degree progression, broaden the participation of students in STEM enrichment, better integrate research and education through improved

New Directions for Higher Education • DOI: 10.1002/he

mentoring and placement, and assess program effectiveness and student outcomes. Like John Jay, Hunter was very conscious about branding the program, changing the name to SciMON to help make the program more accessible and easier to promote.

Partly as a result of having received the I^3 award, Hunter College instituted an overarching Undergraduate Research Initiative and hired a full-time director of UR. The administrators of the I^3 project and the Undergraduate Research Initiative at Hunter were able to obtain additional institutional support from the CUNY Office of Undergraduate Studies, supporting the contention that UR is an appropriate use of university resources in the service of student success.

Offices of Undergraduate Research at York College and the New York City College of Technology.   York College is one of the smallest of the CUNY four-year colleges in terms of total undergraduate enrollment and is the smallest of the three CUNY colleges that has an established OUR. The provost of York College formally announced the launch of a York College Undergraduate Research Program at a CUNY Academic Council meeting in 2010. A full-time faculty member was named as the first director with a physical office and a paid college assistant.

The impetus for creating the OUR emerged in part from the need to support the York College Honors Program. Honors students conduct research for their senior thesis in collaboration with a faculty mentor identified by the OUR. The York OUR also organizes an annual college-wide research day and administers a summer UR experience program funded by the U.S. Department of Education.

At the New York City College of Technology (NYCCT), the OUR was founded in 2011 using institutional funds and currently serves over 450 students every year who engage in research projects. In addition, NYCCT has a faculty-led Undergraduate Research Committee that runs workshops for both students and faculty and has developed a manual to standardize practices across the college. NYCCT is also committed to assessing its own efforts and has received funding from the CUNY central office to assess the impact of the OUR and its programming on student achievement and outcomes.

Among the lessons learned from John Jay, Hunter, York, and NYCCT Colleges are that established physical offices of undergraduate research provide a focal point for both students and faculty. The branding of the PRISM and SciMON initiatives provides an important cognitive touchstone for students seeking to expand their horizons beyond the classroom. John Jay and Hunter Colleges started their UR initiatives as outgrowths of externally funded programs and then received institutional recognition and support when these programs demonstrated successful outcomes for students. The York College and NYCCT offices of undergraduate research were established as a result of college-wide organizational restructuring. More recently, Queens College has appointed a director of undergraduate research and

New Directions for Higher Education • DOI: 10.1002/he

established a new OUR as a direct result of the college's participation in the CUR-sponsored workshops held at CUNY (Malachowski et al., 2010).

Institutional Grants and Programs to Promote Undergraduate Research

Whether or not CUNY colleges have a dedicated office that promotes and coordinates UR efforts, nearly all of the schools have established programs that sponsor students to engage in individual projects with faculty mentors. Institutional resources for these UR programs are rare, with the exception of those described above, and instead rely on external funding. The Louis Stokes Alliances for Minority Participation (LSAMP) program is funded via NSF and sponsors student research at all CUNY schools. Other programs are either specific to one campus or collaborations between two or more colleges.

The minority-serving status of several CUNY schools has also been beneficial for obtaining funding that promotes UR. Both CCNY and Hunter colleges are recipients of National Institutes of Health Research Centers for Minority Institutions grants that fund many different aspects of the research infrastructure in addition to funding individual research efforts by undergraduate students. In partnership with Memorial Sloan Kettering Cancer Center, CCNY has received an NIH U54 program grant that funds cancer research, training, and community outreach. The training component of these large institutional grants is comprehensive and an excellent mechanism for engaging undergraduate students in authentic research projects with real world impact.

The NIH also provides funds for research training and academic support of underrepresented students through its Minority Access to Research Careers (MARC) and Research Initiative for Scientific Enhancement (RISE) programs. Several CUNY schools have been awarded these grants (RISE is specifically for minority-serving institutions) as a way of increasing the number of minority students who engage in biomedical research and pursue careers in this field.

Several major institutional grants that support UR have been awarded to CUNY community colleges. As CUNY community college students frequently transfer to CUNY four-year colleges, developing relationships with senior college faculty via research projects is a positive way to facilitate the transition. Bridges to Baccalaureate grants from the NIH provide a means for community college students to establish relationships with mentors at senior colleges that can be sustained during the transfer process and after (Caplan & MacLachlan, 2014). Queensborough Community College has been a Bridges to Baccalaureate grant recipient since 1995 in partnership with CCNY and Queens College, where many of the students will eventually transfer. Bridges to Baccalaureate grants have also been awarded to La-Guardia Community College in partnership with CCNY and Hunter College and to Medgar Evers College in partnership with Kingsborough Community College.

In addition to the institutional grants described above, the UR enterprise is driven by the faculty themselves via their own research grants, or through NSF-funded Research Experience for Undergraduates (REU) grants. The latter engages groups of students around specific areas of science and can run either during the summer or year round. REUs typically integrate research in a lab with specific discipline-related courses and programming to enhance written and oral communication skills.

Conclusions and Future Steps

The ability of the university to reveal the true power of UR as a high-impact practice requires a synergy between human and financial resources. The CUNY system has been active in this regard, and this chapter has attempted to identify the underlying processes that have enabled this to occur. Chief among these are strong public statements about involving undergraduates in research that each college makes via their PMP reports. The synergy, however, depends on individual faculty to drive initiatives from the "ground up." These initiatives lead to grant support that engages students in a meaningful way; once a record of success has been established, administrative and institutional support often follows.

If our efforts to institutionalize UR are to have a significant impact, however, we need to broaden participation by integrating research into the curriculum. This effort has only just begun. A few NSF-funded models are currently being implemented at CUNY that introduce research activities into the classroom context, but they are restricted to a limited number of disciplines primarily in the sciences. Adequate methods for assessing the impact of these initiatives will be needed as we build toward the goal of having all CUNY students engage in authentic research during their academic careers.

References

Brownell, J. E., & Swaner, L. E. (2010). *Five high-impact educational practices: Research on learning outcomes, completion and quality*. Washington, DC: American Association of Colleges and Universities.

Caplan, A. J., & MacLachlan, E. S. (2014). An overview of undergraduate research in the CUNY community-college system. In N. H. Hensel & B. D. Cejda (Eds.), *Tapping the potential of all: Undergraduate research at community colleges* (pp. 9–16). Washington, DC: Council on Undergraduate Research.

Carpi, A., & Lents, N. L. (2013). Research by undergraduates helps underfinanced colleges as well as students. *Chronicle of Higher Education*. Retrieved from http://chronicle.com/article/How-Undergraduate-Research-Can/142557

Carpi, A., Ronan, D. M., Falconer, H. M., Boyd, H. H., & Lents, N. L. (2013). Development and implementation of targeted STEM retention strategies at a Hispanic-serving institutions. *Journal of Hispanic Higher Education*, 12(3), 280–299.

Eagan, M. K., Hurtado, S., Chang, M. J., Garcia, G. A., Herrera, F. A., & Garibay, J. C. (2013). Making a difference in science education: The impact of undergraduate research programs. *American Education Research Journal, 50,* 683–713.

Graham, M. J., Frederick, J., Byars-Winston, A., Hunter, A.-B., & Handelsman, J. (2013). Increasing persistence of college students in STEM. *Science, 341*(6153), 1455–1456.

Hoskins, S. G., Lopatto, D., & Stevens, L. M. (2011). The C.R.E.A.T.E. approach to primary literature shifts undergraduates' self-assessed ability to read and analyze journal articles, attitudes about science, and epistemological beliefs. *CBE Life Sciences Education, 10*(4), 368–378.

Lopatto, D. (2004). Survey of Undergraduate Research Experiences (SURE): First findings. *Cell Biology Education, 3*(4), 270–277.

Malachowski, M., Ambos, E., Karukstis, K., & Osborn, J. (2010). *Collaborative research: Transformational learning through undergraduate research: Comprehensive support for faculty, institutions, state systems and consortia* (NSF-DUE #0920275, #0920286).

Muth, T. R., & McEntee, C. M. (2014). Undergraduate urban metagenomics research module. *Journal of Microbiology & Biology Educaton, 15*(1), 38–40.

Rabinowitz, V., Nicols-Grinenko, A., Lambe, J., Greenbaum, N., & Gardner, D. (2010). *Building an integrated identification, engagement and assessment infrastructure for STEM enrichment programs at Hunter College* (NSF 0963626).

Russell, S. H., Hancock, M. P., & McCullough, J. (2007). The pipeline: Benefits of undergraduate research experiences. *Science, 316*(5824), 548–549.

Summers, M. F., & Hrabowski, F. A., III. (2006). Diversity: Preparing minority scientists and engineers. *Science, 311*(5769), 1870–1871.

Effie S. MacLachlan is the grants administrator and research programs manager in the Office of the Vice Chancellor for Research, The City University of New York.

Avrom J. Caplan is the associate university dean for research in the Office of the Vice Chancellor for Research, The City University of New York.

New Directions for Higher Education • DOI: 10.1002/he

8

This chapter describes consortial efforts within the Great Lakes Colleges Association to share expertise and programming to build research skills throughout the undergraduate curriculum. Strategies to scaffold research skill development are provided from Allegheny College, Kalamazoo College, and The College of Wooster.

Developing Research Skills Across the Undergraduate Curriculum

Simon Gray, Lee Coates, Ann Fraser, Pam Pierce

Founded in 1962, the Great Lakes Colleges Association (GLCA) is a consortium of 13 private liberal arts colleges in Indiana, Michigan, Ohio, and Pennsylvania. The colleges of the GLCA approach liberal arts learning as an extended engagement with knowledge and lived experience that reaches beyond the notion that education is about the acquisition of practical skills for employment or career advancement. Liberal arts education celebrates the value of learning, nurturing a sense of wonder while developing in students the capacity for inquiry, critical thinking and analysis, and creative expression needed to ask and pursue interesting questions and to share newly acquired knowledge within and beyond the academic community.

There is a conviction within the schools of the GLCA that Undergraduate Research, Scholarship, and Creative Activities (URSCA) and other experiential learning opportunities are especially effective vehicles for preparing students to be creative problem finders and problem solvers. With variations in program implementation, all GLCA campuses have committed significant resources to the design of learning environments that support students as they develop expertise with the cycle of "inquire-research-publish."

A significant expression of this conviction at several GLCA schools is the requirement that all students complete a senior project ("capstone"). Typically completed in the student's major, the senior project has the essential hallmarks of a mentored undergraduate experience: finding a question, acquiring and applying disciplinary knowledge and methods, working independently with responsibility for the project's design, and communicating the project's results. These experiences provide the benefits associated with URSCA (Kinzie, 2013; Schermer & Gray, 2012).

NEW DIRECTIONS FOR HIGHER EDUCATION, no. 169, Spring 2015 © 2015 Wiley Periodicals, Inc.
Published online in Wiley Online Library (wileyonlinelibrary.com) • DOI: 10.1002/he.20125

A Broad Definition of URSCA

The Council on Undergraduate Research (CUR) defines undergraduate research (UR) as "An inquiry or investigation conducted by an undergraduate student that makes an original intellectual or creative contribution to the discipline." While this is the ideal outcome for URSCA experiences and for all senior projects, here we adopt a broader definition from Willison and O'Regan (2007), which sees student involvement with research as "a continuum of knowledge production, from knowledge new to the learner to knowledge new to humankind, moving from the commonly known, to the commonly not known, to the totally unknown" (p. 394).

This definition is in step with the liberal arts goal of moving students from knowledge consumers to knowledge producers, and it acknowledges that this transformation must occur in stages that must be supported through carefully designed structures that emphasize integration, iteration, and collaboration (Smith, 2007). While not all senior projects rise to CUR's standard, these projects do result in valuable learning and developmental gains. In a three-year study of required senior projects at four liberal arts schools, Schermer and Gray (2012) concluded that students of all levels of ability benefited from their senior project experience independently of the project's originality and its contribution to the field.

Developing URSCA Skills

The Research Skill Development Framework developed by Willison and O'Regan (2007) identified six facets of the research process that students must develop: (a) identifying questions to pursue, (b) applying appropriate methods to collect data/information, (c and d) evaluating and organizing data, (e) synthesizing and analyzing collected data, and (f) communicating the results with an awareness of the associated ethical and social issues. These skills exist across a continuum, with the simpler skills having a lower level of interdependency than the skills of critical thinking, analysis, and emotional intelligence (Walkington et al., 2011).

The development of these skills occurs through repeated and differentiated exposure to research and research-like experiences. This happens through coursework (in the general education curriculum and the major), cocurricular and extracurricular opportunities (mentored UR, internships, service learning, and study away), a set of allied resources (libraries, information technology, writing center, learning center, and career planning), and opportunities to share what has been learned (publication, conferences, and celebration days). All GLCA campuses have an office that promotes and coordinates URSCA opportunities encompassing most of the elements identified in CUR's *Characteristics of Excellence in Undergraduate Research* (Hensel, 2012).

Consortial Involvement—GLCA Programming

The GLCA's mission is to be a leading force on behalf of education in the tradition of the liberal arts and to take actions that strengthen its colleges. Thus, GLCA programs seek to foster collaborations that leverage the consortium's expertise in a way that leads to benefits individual campuses would find difficult to achieve alone. Three programs that have impacted URSCA on GLCA campuses are representative of this philosophy.

GLCA Expanding Collaboration Initiative. Launched in 2013 with funding from the Andrew W. Mellon Foundation, this program supports the development of multicampus communities of practice, allowing them to share expertise, develop joint programs, bring new perspectives to current courses, and creatively engage in new realms of thinking. One Expanding Collaboration project brought together the computer science faculty from three GLCA campuses to identify the knowledge and skills needed for computer science UR and their development through courses within the major. In another project, neuroscience faculty and summer research students from five GLCA campuses visited the participating campuses to train on the specialized research methods and techniques used in their labs, providing professional development for students and faculty. The GLCA has hosted two Digital Liberal Arts meetings that led to a range of developing Expanding Collaboration projects, including *Oral History and Digital Storytelling*, a collaborative of faculty from seven GLCA schools to establish a community of practice for GLCA faculty interested in oral history and digital storytelling for faculty–student research, cross-institutional collaboration, and community engagement. The *Digital Scholar Program* seeks to combine the traditional skill development of a liberal arts education with new digital literacies to build sustainable capacity for digital projects and to better prepare students for their careers. *Mapping the Megalopolis* is a faculty–student research project seeking to explore the fundamental question of how something as immediate and local as place is produced/reproduced within a setting such as Mexico City, one of the great megalopolises of the 21st century.

GLCA CUR STEM Workshops. As a participant in CUR's project to institutionalize UR within systems and consortia (Malachowski, Ambos, Karukstis, & Osborn, 2010), the GLCA participated in two workshops to further strengthen UR within science, technology, engineering, and math (STEM) disciplines throughout the consortium. One outcome of the workshops was the creation of the GLCA Undergraduate Research and Scholarly Activity Advisory Board to promote sharing and collaboration across GLCA campuses. The board's makeup reflects the intellectual diversity of scholarship and research found on a liberal arts campus. The board holds monthly virtual meetings to discuss areas of interest and to share what is happening on each campus. The board has identified several areas of broad interest, including integration of research-like experiences into introductory courses, best practices for training faculty to serve as effective mentors and for assessing mentoring quality, increasing access to URSCA experiences by underrepresented groups, and broadening URSCA experiences beyond the STEM fields. While physical meetings are always productive, the GLCA is increasingly relying on low-cost video conferences to gather information and to initiate and sustain collaboration. The Advisory Board will use a series of webinars on topics of interest to inform the campuses of the ideas being considered, to collect additional thoughts on them, and to gauge interest in pursuing an Expanding Collaboration project around one or more topic.

GLCA Lattice for Pedagogical Research and Practice.   The Lattice program was created in January 2012 with support from the Teagle Foundation. Building on the success of an earlier Teagle-funded project, the Pathways to Learning Collegium, the Lattice program is designed to stir a greater commitment among faculty to work with colleagues on improving pedagogical effectiveness and to develop a stronger sense of teaching as a scholarly endeavor based on research on human learning. The program established a core of Teagle Pedagogy Fellows, faculty members who combine knowledge of the research on human learning with an understanding of how these principles could inform alternative approaches to undergraduate pedagogy. During the two-year program, pairs of Pedagogy Fellows traveled to member colleges for Colloquies on Pedagogical Research and Practice. At these meetings, the Pedagogy Fellows facilitated conversations on pedagogy in support of effective teaching and learning within different college environments.

Recognizing that our institutions benefit by addressing these challenges as a group, the Pedagogy Fellows envisioned that the natural successor to the Lattice program would be a GLCA Consortial Center for Teaching and Learning.

Case Studies of Undergraduate Research Development Throughout the Curriculum

As illustrations of particular strategies to scaffold research skill development throughout the curriculum, three models are presented from Allegheny College, Kalamazoo College, and The College of Wooster.

The Capstone Senior Project at Allegheny College.   Since its founding in 1815, Allegheny College has required all graduates to complete a capstone, which over time has evolved into an independent research project conducted during a student's senior year in the department of the student's major. Called the "Senior Project," this experience has become an integral component of the Allegheny College culture with implications for the design of curricula (general education and departmental) that prepare students.

Scaffolding of Skills for the Senior Project: Writing, Speaking, and Critical Thinking.   The Allegheny College curriculum includes five courses, FS-101, FS-102, FS-201, junior seminar, and senior project that are required for graduation for all students and provide the backbone of the Allegheny educational experience. The First-Year/Sophomore Seminar (FS) courses focus on speaking and writing. Students are also required to complete a major, a minor in a division different from that of the major, and "distribution courses" from outside the divisions of the major and minor. While courses taken for the major and minor provide students with breadth and depth in specific content areas in addition to skills, the FS courses, junior seminar, and senior project are designed to focus on skills and process.

The goal for FS-101 is to familiarize first-semester students with the conventions of description and summary in writing and speaking. The goal for FS-102 is to consider research and argument in writing and speaking. In addition, students learn to locate, critically evaluate, interpret, and discuss resource materials, and are expected to support their ideas in presentations and writing assignments with secondary sources.

During the sophomore year, students take an FS-201 class that emphasizes writing and oral communication within a discipline. Some departments require majors to take a departmental FS-201 in order to learn the research and writing conventions specific to their discipline.

After completing an FS-201 course and declaring a major, a student enrolls in a department-specific junior seminar that serves as the bridge between the FS courses and the senior project. As described in the college catalogue (Catalogue 2013–2014, 2013), these junior seminars "develop the student's ability to engage in advanced scholarship and communication in a discipline" and emphasize "methods of scholarship, the process of independent inquiry, and oral, written, and/or other (e.g., visual) communication skills" (p. 8). Particularly in the social and natural sciences, the junior seminar serves as the launching point for senior project ideas. A recent study of capstones (Schermer & Gray, 2012), funded by the Teagle Foundation, found that Allegheny students in the natural sciences reported that the junior seminar prepared them well for the senior project. This was not the case for some of the nonscience disciplines, which has led to efforts to improve the junior seminar experience for all students.

Noncurricular Structures and Opportunities That Support the Senior Project.   The Allegheny College curriculum has been carefully designed to develop skills a student needs for the senior project. Additionally, several noncurricular structures have been developed to support the curriculum and senior project. For example, reference librarians play a large support role for students during the senior project process, particularly for students doing projects in the humanities.

Allegheny students have additional opportunities to participate in faculty research or other creative activities prior to their senior year. Students may enroll in "independent study" courses where they work with faculty on research projects and begin to get research and laboratory experience. In some cases, these students help senior project students with their research thereby learning about the senior project process, while the senior students get help with their projects and gain valuable peer-to-peer mentoring experience. Students also have the opportunity to participate in research projects with Allegheny faculty during the summer. These projects are funded by the Provost Office through endowed funds or research grants (NSF, NIH, HHMI, and Mellon Foundation). Because students receive a stipend for summer research and enroll in the senior project course during their senior year, students may not work directly on their senior research project during the summer. However, students can work on summer research projects that use similar techniques as the senior project research or can collect preliminary data to help them refine protocols for their senior project.

To disseminate, celebrate, and reinforce Allegheny's curricular emphasis on oral communications, the URSCA office has developed several campus-wide events where students can present their results. In addition to a fall semester poster symposium for students to present their summer research projects and a spring semester poster symposium that celebrates the completion of the senior project, the Allegheny College Research Seminar Series (ACRoSS) was developed (ACRoSS, 2013). ACRoSS is a weekly summer meeting for students to present their projects to an audience of administrators, faculty, and other research students. During the summer of 2013, 58 students from 16 departments and programs presented their projects to an audience that averaged 120 attendees. The Provost Office also provides travel funds for students who present their research at regional and national conferences.

The Senior Individualized Project at Kalamazoo College. Undergraduate research at Kalamazoo College is institutionalized through the "Senior Individualized Project" (SIP), a major independent research or creative project that all students must undertake. The SIP requirement has been in place for over 50 years and represents the capstone of the college's liberal arts education program. Students complete their projects under the direction of a mentor on campus or at another institution, and each project is overseen and evaluated by a faculty member in the sponsoring department at Kalamazoo College. This capstone experience is a culture shaper, encouraging students to think deeply about their interests and to be more intentional in their academic and technical preparation for this in-depth work. Preparation for the SIP occurs across the four years through various avenues, including general education and discipline-specific coursework, faculty–student research or creative activity collaborations, study away, service learning, and career exploration opportunities. These cumulative experiences prepare students to chart the direction of their senior project, take ownership of the project, and follow it through to completion and dissemination.

Preparation for the SIP.   Preparation for independent scholarship is institutionalized through a First-Year Seminar that all entering students take in fall of the first year and continues with a required Sophomore Seminar. While subject matter for each seminar section varies with the instructor's discipline and interests, all seminars are developed around common programmatic components and learning goals. These include frequent discussion, reading and writing exercises that promote development of critical thinking skills, intercultural proficiency, communication proficiency, and information literacy.

First-year seminars include a mandatory research component called "Beyond Google" that helps students learn how to conceive and hone a research topic; how to develop and substantiate arguments; and how to locate, evaluate, and cite sources. Development of student writing and research skills is further supported through a campus Writing Center and Research Consultant Center. Sophomore seminars continue to build on critical thinking and communication skills while challenging students to dive deeper into differentiating between observation and interpretation. These seminars also explore crossing boundaries of difference, especially in relation to cultural differences and traditions in order to prepare students for advanced work in a major, for study abroad, and for independent scholarship required for the SIP.

Undergraduates declare an academic major midway through the sophomore year, but most are still far from identifying the area of focus for their SIP research. Required and elective coursework associated within the major plays an important role in helping students envision the type of research they would like to conduct and in providing them with the knowledge and skills needed to undertake the project.

Ideally, students will have taken a number of upper level courses prior to conducting the SIP, but the reality is more complicated owing to the high percentage (over 70%) of students that participate in a three- to six-month study-abroad experience, typically in their junior year. Consequently, a number of departments (e.g., biology, chemistry, physics, mathematics, economics, business, English, and foreign languages) use a core curriculum to prepare their majors for the SIP and encourage students to get in one or more upper level courses relevant to their SIP area before the summer of their junior year. Some departments (e.g., anthropology and sociology, art and art history, classics, history, psychology, and religion) have developed single courses specifically designed to prepare students for SIP-level work in the discipline. These research methods and theory courses are typically not focused on a particular topic, as upper level electives are, but instead use development and planning of the SIP topic as the central focus for the course so that students can use the framework of the course to hone their SIP plans. These courses are typically taken in the junior year and are usually required for majors and any nonmajor intending to conduct an SIP in that discipline.

Experiential opportunities outside the classroom also challenge students to develop skills as independent thinkers, problem solvers, and communicators, helping them prepare for their SIP experience. Nearly all students at Kalamazoo participate in at least one of the following college opportunities: course-embedded cocurricular service-learning projects with local schools or community-based organizations, extracurricular service-learning opportunities organized through the college's Service Learning Institute and certain student organizations, and career exploration opportunities with alumni that are brokered through the college's Center for Career and Professional Development. All of these opportunities allow students to connect theory with practice while accumulating knowledge and skills that may be useful during their SIP. Many students also participate in summer internships prior to conducting their SIP. This may be through research with a faculty member on our campus, most commonly in the sciences, or through internship programs or individual arrangements with other institutions, with limited pools of support funds. A final important experience that prepares students for the SIP is study abroad. The life skills that students build while navigating the landscape, language, and cultures of a foreign country lead to considerable growth in their problem-solving abilities and their ability to adapt to uncertainty and the unknown. Most students return with a much heightened sense of self-confidence and a set of life skills that serve them well in their personal life as well as in the SIP arena.

Conception and Completion of the SIP.   By the end of the junior year, students are generally well prepared to undertake the major independent work that will become their SIP. Students have considerable agency in determining the area and direction of their SIP but must obtain approval from a sponsoring department before beginning their work. Most science SIPs are conducted in established research labs, either on our campus or at other institutions, and students largely determine the direction of their SIP work by seeking out specific labs with a focus in the student's area of interest. In departments in which students conduct literature-based SIPs, or combine this with a job shadowing opportunity, the SIP topic is often developed in association with a junior seminar course or in consultation with a specific faculty member. In all departments, students are provided with guidelines on the content, format, and deadlines for specific components. Students then meet periodically with their supervising professor, and sometimes a peer group, to review progress, receive feedback, and discuss revisions. Biology and some other departments use activities associated with a separate Senior Seminar course for this review process and public presentation of the work (Moore, Dueweke, Newton, & Stevens-Truss, 2005).

Senior Independent Study at The College of Wooster.   The College of Wooster has, over a period of more than 60 years, developed a rigorous program of study that culminates with a senior research experience. The Senior Independent Study Project ("Senior IS") is the hallmark of the Wooster curriculum. We ask our seniors to become explorers and cocreators of knowledge as they progress through a year-long research project working one-on-one with a faculty member in their major. Senior IS has shaped our curriculum and has effectively created a "culture of research" that guides how we teach our introductory and mid-level courses. In fact, the entire curriculum is strategically designed to gradually build students' experiences with research and research-like activities so that each student is prepared for a significant, year-long senior research experience.

To be prepared for this capstone experience, students need the content knowledge provided within the major as well as a research-focused set of skills and dispositions. Students need to know where the resources are across campus and how to access them. They need to develop the habits of mind that allow them to ask important questions and to persevere as they seek answers.

Student preparation begins in the first semester as each student is required to enroll in a First-Year Seminar. Although the topic of each seminar is different, each seminar is small (15–16 students) and writing intensive. The faculty member introduces students to the process of critical thinking so that students learn to question statements, to state an opinion, and to support a thesis. Instructors require students to peer edit the work of other students, and several papers go through multiple drafts.

Students will build upon this knowledge in a second writing-intensive course, which is taken during semesters two through five of a student's eight-semester experience. Most students will take this required writing-intensive course within their major, which allows them to focus on writing in their field. By the time students have completed this second writing-intensive course, we expect that they have developed strong abilities in the area of written expression.

As students progress through the major, they encounter the "research-as-pedagogy" approach that our faculty knows will enhance the student learning experience. For example, a student in an introductory psychology or introductory statistics course might be asked to formulate a small research question that could be addressed through a short experiment. This small-scale investigation can be done as early as the introductory-level courses, and it gets students prepared to ask interesting questions and to think about how to answer them.

Our Sophomore Research Program enables students to work with a faculty member, for pay, on a research project initiated by the faculty member. Most of these projects occur during the academic year, with students working from two to five hours per week on research and meetings. Funds are also available for summer Sophomore Research projects. The nature of these projects varies widely across the disciplines. In every instance, a student will gain valuable experience and learn about the work involved in pursuing research within a discipline.

Wooster students are encouraged to pursue research experiences in the summer. These Sophomore Research and Summer Research opportunities are some of the best vehicles for helping students to understand the nature of research and to develop some of the skills and habits of mind necessary for a deep investigation. By scaffolding elements of research on a small scale in courses, we have been able to successfully bring all students to where they need to be as they begin their Senior IS. Throughout the senior year, Wooster students are involved in genuine research projects at all levels. The best of these projects would rival a master's thesis, and the students pursue a new avenue of inquiry with their own unique perspective.

References

ACRoSS. (2013). *Allegheny college research seminar series.* Retrieved from http://sites .allegheny.edu/research/across-2013/

Catalogue 2013–2014. (2013). *Allegheny college catalogue 2013–2014.* Retrieved from http://sitesmedia.s3.amazonaws.com/academics/files/2013/08/full-catalogue.pdf

Hensel, N. (Ed.). (2012). *Characteristics of excellence in undergraduate research (COEUR).* Washington, DC: Council on Undergraduate Research.

Kinzie, J. (2013). Taking stock of capstones and integrative learning. *Peer Review, 15*(4), 27–30.

Malachowski, M., Ambos, E., Karukstis, K., & Osborn, J. (2010). *Collaborative research: Transformational learning through undergraduate research: Comprehensive support for faculty, institutions, state systems and consortia* (NSF-DUE #0920275, #0920286).

Moore, D. B., Dueweke, A., Newton, C. R., & Stevens-Truss, R. (2005). Mentoring students in professional-quality science communication. *Council on Undergraduate Research Quarterly,* March, 118–121.

Schermer, T., & Gray, S. (2012). *The senior capstone: Transformative experiences in the liberal arts. Final report to the Teagle Foundation.* Retrieved from http://www .teaglefoundation.org/teagle/media/library/documents/resources/Augustana-Final -Report.pdf

Smith, E. (2007). Integrating information and scientific research skills training within a research-supportive undergraduate curriculum. In K. Karukstis & T. Elgren (Eds.), *Developing & sustaining a research-supportive curriculum: A compendium of successful practices* (pp. 137–174). Washington, DC: Council on Undergraduate Research.

Walkington, H., Griffin, A., Keys-Mathews, L., Metoyer, S., Miller, W., Baker, R., & France, D. (2011). Embedding research-based learning early in the undergraduate geography curriculum. *Journal of Geography in Higher Education, 35*(3), 315–330.

Willison, J., & O'Regan, K. (2007). Commonly known, commonly not known, totally unknown: A framework for students becoming researchers. *Higher Education Research & Development, 26*(4), 393–409.

SIMON GRAY *is an associate professor of computer science at The College of Wooster.*

LEE COATES *is a professor of biology, neuroscience, and global health studies, and the director of the URSCA Office at Allegheny College.*

ANN FRASER *is an associate professor of biology at Kalamazoo College.*

PAM PIERCE *is a professor of mathematics at The College of Wooster.*

9

In this final chapter, we summarize the lessons learned from working with six systems/consortia to enhance and expand undergraduate research. The theory of change model for systems/consortia differs in significant ways from the change processes exhibited by individual institutions, offering important insights for academic leaders as they seek to leverage educational change effectively.

Fostering Undergraduate Research Change at the System and Consortium Level: Perspectives From the Council on Undergraduate Research

Mitchell Malachowski, Jeffrey M. Osborn, Kerry K. Karukstis, Elizabeth L. Ambos, Shontay L. Kincaid, Daniel Weiler

The Council on Undergraduate Research (CUR) is a national organization with over 10,000 individual and 700 institutional members representing over 900 colleges/universities of all types. Ongoing requests from institutions for opportunities to engage in intensive reflection and discussions around institutionalizing undergraduate research (UR) led to the focus of CUR's Workshop Program for State Systems and Consortia funded by the National Science Foundation (Malachowski, Ambos, Karukstis, & Osborn, 2010). The history and scope of the workshop program are summarized in Chapter 1 of this volume.

The perspectives shared in this chapter draw on lessons learned from working with The California State University System (CSU), University of Wisconsin System (UW), Council of Public Liberal Arts Colleges (COPLAC), City University of New York System (CUNY), Great Lakes Colleges Association (GLCA), and Pennsylvania State System of Higher Education (PASSHE). Over a five-year period, CUR also sought to better understand the national landscape of UR, develop national models of success for higher education systems with an emphasis on UR, and help system/consortium offices leverage resources to connect UR experiences with established pathways of success. To this end, NSF granted CUR a

NEW DIRECTIONS FOR HIGHER EDUCATION, no. 169, Spring 2015 © 2015 Wiley Periodicals, Inc.
Published online in Wiley Online Library (wileyonlinelibrary.com) • DOI: 10.1002/he.20126

WIDER (Widening Implementation and Demonstration of Evidence-based Reforms) supplement to study the culture of each system and develop an understanding of how change occurs at the system/consortium level.

Our engagement with each system/consortium began with interviews of system administrators to identify priorities and initiatives. We also assessed the strengths and shortcomings of each system/consortium and each of their member campuses, using detailed inventory questionnaires and self-studies. These were subsequently used to develop customized workshops and follow-up activities for each system/consortium, giving us the opportunity to deeply work within each system's/consortium's culture.

Following our engagement with each of the systems/consortia, we convened a summit meeting for all six systems/consortia and their member campuses to maximize engagement with the broader community of participants and stakeholders. The summit afforded participants the opportunity to learn about the working environment of each system and understand shared challenges. The summit also provided attendees with a chance to engage, network, and exchange information across the systems/consortia as a means to further sustain progress that they made toward institutionalizing UR. Moreover, as part of the project, we provided training opportunities for faculty and administrators from the systems/consortia to develop their skills to serve as facilitators, provide avenues for leadership development, and further sustain their ability to lead the cultural and organization change needed on their campuses and across their systems/consortia.

Bringing Undergraduate Research to Scale: What Works (and What Doesn't) in Institutionalizing Undergraduate Research Within Systems and Consortia?

Some key reflections from our work with the six systems/consortia and their member campuses to institutionalize UR, including lessons learned about what works (and what doesn't), are shared in the following section from the campus and the system/consortium perspectives.

Campus Perspectives.   As part of our efforts, we performed extensive evaluations and assessments of the outcomes from the workshops and the campus activities. The results of these assessments informed many of our activities and provided a road map for the subsequent work of the participant teams and system/consortium offices. So, what did the evaluations tell us about the campuses? First, the workshop model was successful in providing the participants with valuable information about UR and helped them in developing their own plans for campus implementation. The goals that were generated at the workshops commonly included items such as defining and inventorying campus UR, establishing UR offices and faculty/staff champions and advocates, creating UR celebrations, infusing UR into the curriculum, and incentivizing and funding UR activities. There were also many campuses that wanted to build UR into faculty workload, find better ways to assess student and faculty outcomes, integrate UR within already existing campus activities, or find ways to connect UR to community-based activities.

Once they returned to campus, most teams reported that their campus had successfully undertaken a variety of UR implementation measures, including the establishment of a campus UR office, building research into the curriculum, collaborations with other universities, establishment of a mentor reward program, and providing student grants for UR activities, along with other measures. Many described how UR had been initiated not only in many STEM-related departments but also in many non-STEM departments.

At the same time, many workshop teams continued to report the persistence of a number of obstacles, including a lack of senior administrator support, weak faculty buy-in, no UR program budget, no strategy for incorporating UR into courses, and no workload adjustments. Respondents were particularly concerned with resource limitations, constraints on both faculty and student time, issues of faculty motivation, and efforts to integrate UR into curricula. Some strategies pursued had been previously identified by workshop participants as likely to "work best" on their campuses (e.g., establishing a campus UR office and integrating UR into faculty workload requirements). What many of the strategies had in common is that they would require a high degree of faculty–administrator consensus on the value of UR and a determined effort to change established academic and administrative values and procedures.

It is interesting to consider that many of the obstacles cited—lack of faculty motivation, constraints on faculty time, absence of workload accommodations—reflect the lack of a "business" model for UR, as noted in the California State University account in Chapter 3 of this volume. While high-impact practices like UR certainly enhance student learning and contribute to faculty satisfaction as well as scholarship, long-term sustainability of UR as a central component of undergraduate education will require that institutions and systems find ways to compensate faculty for their efforts. Redefinitions of faculty workload beyond standard course-load designations, recognition of UR in tenure/promotion criteria, and incorporation of UR into the curriculum are all effective measures that institutions in this project have implemented. Nevertheless, a much broader adoption of such practices will be necessary to achieve system-wide success (e.g., Hensel & Paul, 2012).

There is another issue that is key to many of the campus success stories. The many demands on faculty time and turnover among faculty, leadership teams, and administrators make it difficult for campuses to maintain momentum in their efforts to scale up and institutionalize UR. One strategy that shows promise for protecting institutional memory and guiding UR implementation is the establishment of a central campus office charged with pursuing those goals. Ideally, a campus director of UR would have a governing board and administration mandate, connections to sources of assistance and advice like CUR, resources for supporting students and faculty, and a strategic plan with built-in reporting requirements to ensure that UR implementations stay on track. Establishment and support of such an office could help to focus implementation efforts, provide a clear signal of administrative priorities, and become an important component of efforts to foster a campus culture of support for UR. As one system-level administrator told us, "Without someone who will fight for UR resources, competing claims will dominate."

System- and Consortium-Level Perspectives. While the primary responsibility for UR implementation is lodged at the campus level, system/consortium-level administrators play key roles in helping their campuses overcome obstacles and maintain implementation momentum. It is clear that increased effectiveness at the system/consortium level will not come through mandates, top-down directives do not work, and the system/consortium-level authority for such matters is often ambiguous at best. Instead, system administrators endorsed collaboration, coordination, and information dissemination. They favored the development of strategies to resolve issues of UR and faculty workload, thought more workshops would help, and were clear that for UR to become institutionalized it would have to be seen as a standard component of the instructional repertoire rather than an "add-on." They were particularly aware of the limits of their authority and resources, understood that they were in no position to issue mandates, but believed that they could be helpful by, for example, identifying expert advisors, obtaining good impact data, coordinating campus efforts, supporting relevant campus performance measures, disseminating models of success, helping to build cooperation among campuses, and providing support for including UR in faculty performance measures.

Leaders at this level can endorse ideas and encourage action; highlight UR in explanations and interpretations of system/consortium mission statements and planning documents; make the UR case to governing boards, legislatures, and other funding agencies; help to coordinate campus interactions; obtain and disseminate information; identify and engage expert assistance; arrange various forms of professional development and networking; and work to obtain additional resources. As one system-level administrator suggested, every campus should identify one person who could be a principal liaison for UR to the system/consortium level. This would provide system/consortium administrators with detailed information about the progress of UR through a key point of contact on each campus. Collectively, the liaisons would serve as a body of advisors who could help with an array of system/consortium-level UR activities.

Toward a Robust Theory of Change Model for Systems and Consortia: Insights From the CUR Professional Development Model

At a time when the value of the college experience is being intensively questioned, Gagliardi, Martin, Wise, and Blaich point out in Chapter 2 of this volume that academic leaders are searching for strategies that can express, enhance, and cost-effectively grow the value of an undergraduate education. As we have described in Chapter 1 of this volume, UR is such a strategy that adds significant value to student learning and can be effectively scaled if it is firmly seated in the culture, curriculum, and reward systems of an institution.

Assessments of the workshop program for systems/consortia clearly demonstrate the value of the CUR curricula, team planning, and intensive coaching provided to the six systems/consortia. The project's evaluation provided insights as to what worked well for systems/consortia to grow and develop their UR programs and where challenges were encountered.

But even in the face of the extraordinary evidence of UR's value, and with the commitments of the six systems/consortia to work together and with CUR to effect lasting change, transformation occurs slowly. Kotter (2012) contends that at least eight areas of sequential action are essential for transformative change: (a) a sense of urgency must be established; (b) a guiding coalition must be created; (c) a clear vision and strategy must be presented; (d) stakeholders must communicate the change vision; (e) participants must be empowered to broad-based action; (f) short-term wins are generated and celebrated; (g) participants consolidate gains, produce more change; and (h) new approaches are thoroughly embedded in the culture.

CUR's experience working with over 450 institutions since 1996, including the 80 institutions engaged in the system/consortium project, is that we believe all eight of these stages were undertaken by the six systems/consortia with whom we worked. The eighth element—embedding in the culture—is the single most important stumbling block, however, that campuses and systems face in instituting transformational and sustained change. Our experience reaffirms the extensive literature on higher education change (e.g., Kezar, 2009), including studies by the American Council on Education (Eckel, Green, & Hill, 2001; Eckel, Green, Hill, & Mallon, 1999). Consistent with Kotter's (2012) work, findings by Eckel et al. showed that the most important factor in systemic change initiatives is the role of campus leaders, both administrators and faculty members. The singular importance of leadership is interwoven through all eight sequential steps in Kotter's change process. Leaders must make a clear and compelling case for change, and they must articulate this case early, publicly, and frequently if the transformation is to be sustained. Effective change leaders develop supporting structures, create incentives, and provide resources.

NEW DIRECTIONS FOR HIGHER EDUCATION • DOI: 10.1002/he

System and consortium leaders are often without a well-developed "road map" to guide their work on transformational change with respect to UR, however. How do the results from CUR's work with systems/consortia illumine a specific theory of UR change model for systems/consortia, a clear "road map," as it were? CUR has a well-established theory of change model for individual institutions, which is framed by the *Characteristics of Excellence in Undergraduate Research* document (Hensel, 2012) described in Chapter 1 of this volume. What are the differences between an individual campus change process that follows these precepts and a broader system-based change approach?

Our first conclusion is that system/consortial change processes exhibit distinct differences to models developed for individual campuses. Following the suggestions of Taplin and Clark (2012), we developed a matrix to compare and contrast the conditions needed to effect transformative change in UR, both at the individual campus level and for a system/consortium as a whole. Table 9.1 outlines the 12 "Conditions for Change to Occur," deemed the domains essential for high-quality UR, taken from CUR's *Characteristics of Excellence in Undergraduate Research* (Hensel, 2012).

Although there are similarities between some of the conditions necessary for transformative change at the individual and system/consortium level, there are significant differences as well. For example, consider the domain of "recognition," which refers primarily to the need for campuses to reward faculty tangibly for UR mentorship. If the campus is to transform to a high-quality UR environment, all of the heavy lifting to achieve that condition is at the campus level. System/consortium offices rarely have a role in hiring or retaining faculty and thus would not be involved in direct faculty rewards.

Conversely, there are several domains for systems/consortia to achieve excellence in UR that can, and should, be strongly facilitated by system/consortium offices, using the "soft" powers of convening, connecting, and communicating. These include professional development, external funding, dissemination, assessment, and, in some instances, research infrastructure.

Implications for Internal and External Stakeholders Regarding Investments in Undergraduate Research

The results of our work with systems/consortia and their campuses have some clear implications for the types of investments that need to be made to effectively institutionalize UR in ways that are enduring for the long term.

Change at the System/Consortium-Level Requires Long-Term Investment.   As articulated throughout this volume and summarized in this chapter, the change processes that occur at the system/consortium level are distinctly different than the models of change that unfold at the institutional level. The students, faculty, and staff who learn and work within the

Table 9.1. The Conditions for Change to Occur

Condition for Change to Occur	Individual Campus	System/Consortium
Campus mission and culture	Formal commitment of institution to UR; integration with other high-impact practices; all disciplines participate, students can access UR easily, faculty are scholarly and committed to engage undergraduates in research	Formal commitment of system/consortium to UR as a positive practice, faculty encouraged to involve undergraduates in research; less specific than campus mission and culture as systems/consortia usually represent diverse institutions
Administrative support	UR program offices; funding for faculty and students; faculty assignment includes research; staff support, etc.	Little direct engagement, unless system/consortium policy changes would help
Research infrastructure	Dedicated space, equipment, libraries, and other research support exist	Little direct engagement, except in shared digital resources (libraries) that can be connected via systems/consortia Internet-based processes
Professional development	Research training; sabbatical leaves; other forms of professional development exist	Act as a convenor and connector for professional development. Central role, particularly in tight budgets
Recognition	Faculty and staff retention, tenure, and promotion guidelines support UR	Little direct engagement, unless system/consortium policy changes would help
External funding	Culture that supports and promotes faculty and administrators seeking external funding for UR	Systems/consortia may be able to divert funds held centrally to share among campuses; may be able to leverage additional funds (particularly state funds). Central role, particularly to state/regional stakeholders
Dissemination	Presentation of UR outcomes on campus and at professional meetings	Presentation at system/consortium-wide conference, Board of Trustees, etc. Central role, particularly to external stakeholders
Student-centered issues	Scaffolded UR experiences that are developmentally appropriate exist; UR student learning communities, peer/near-peer mentors are fostered; connections to extracurricular activities, student life, and development exist	Little direct engagement; unless system/consortium policy changes would help

(Continued)

New Directions for Higher Education • DOI: 10.1002/he

Table 9.1. Continued

Condition for Change to Occur	Individual Campus	System/Consortium
Curriculum	Faculty and student incentives to change to developmentally integrate research into curricula exist; flexible scheduling, training, etc.	Little direct engagement; unless system/consortium policy changes would help. Act as a convenor and connector for professional development, system/consortium-wide workshops, grant program, etc.
Summer research programs	Faculty and student compensation, housing, infrastructure, symposia are provided	Little direct engagement; unless system/consortium policy changes would help
Assessment	Student learning outcomes defined; UR program assessment takes place	Student performance outcomes defined, particularly system/consortia student retention and graduation. Central role, particularly for aggregate data
Strategic planning	UR formally included	UR formally included

system/consortium and their member campuses as well as the broad spectrum of external stakeholders (e.g., associations, funding agencies, and governing boards) need to be mindful of these differences, including some of the theoretical context that underpins these change processes. Moreover, at the scale of systems/consortia, the time horizon for the types of organizational and cultural changes that are needed to truly institutionalize UR will take longer than that at the individual campus level. Although strategically focused efforts like CUR's work with the six systems/consortia (Malachowski et al., 2010) outlined in this volume can catalyze the pace of change, internal and external stakeholders need to be reminded about the influence of scale and encouraged to support and to fund change processes over longer time frames.

Investing in Teams and a Nested Leadership Model. It is clear from our work with the six systems/consortia to institutionalize UR that leaders matter a great deal and that there are particular leadership strategies that are most effective in the system/consortium context. In particular, system/consortium offices are encouraged to first invest in a deep and intentional review of the team envisioned to lead and oversee the effort. The team selected should include multiple leaders that will provide a nested, or redundant, leadership model. Each team member needs to be identified, and clearly defined principles and assignments for each person need to be developed. Furthermore, the leadership team (and key stakeholders) need assurance from the highest levels of the system/consortium that this leadership structure will be maintained. This structure doesn't have to include the same people, but there needs to be a long-term commitment to empower and support whoever is tasked with the effort.

We have required the participation of a team from the system/consortium office as well as a team from each member institution. Each team consists of at least one administrative leader with resource allocation responsibility. Such leadership is an important element for sustained change (Kezar, 2009). For organizations to initiate and sustain change, there is ample evidence that team members must have a shared vision, use a systems approach that recognizes the interrelationships among participants, and learn as a team particularly through personal commitments made to each other (Henderson, Beach, & Finkelstein, 2011; Senge, Kleiner, Roberts, Ross, & Smith, 1994). Furthermore, participation involving faculty (and/or staff) from multiple disciplines in discourse and activities focused on faculty development lead to more creative approaches (Frost & Jean, 2003; Lynd-Balta, Erklenz-Watts, Freeman, & Westbay, 2006). The collaborative team model invokes a stronger commitment to the goals and a greater appreciation of the dedication of colleagues to the long-range objectives (Carstens & Howell, 2012). Additionally, a network both inside and outside of the team's own institution (i.e., across the system/consortium) to collaborate with and to disseminate results, as well as share progress and challenges, is also a critical factor in achieving and sustaining long-term success (Sunal et al., 2001). These same principles hold true for UR, as CUR has confirmed these findings through the evaluation of our workshop program.

Investing in the Institutionalization of Undergraduate Research via Synergy.   For systems/consortia and their member campuses to truly realize the full benefits of UR, it should not be considered a stand-alone "project" or "initiative." Rather, systems/consortia should strive to institutionalize UR in ways that weave it into the "fabric" of their learning environments through a broad range of synergistic connections.

It is clear that deep student engagement can occur through an array of high-impact curricular and cocurricular experiences (Kuh, 2008; Kuh, Kinzie, Schuh, Whitt, & Associates, 2005; Kuh & O'Donnell, 2013), but many consider UR to be "first among equals" of the high-impact practices because UR can simultaneously achieve student, faculty, institutional, and system/consortium outcomes. Most importantly, UR provides the most natural, and perhaps best, opportunity for the majority of faculty members to deeply engage students (Osborn & Karukstis, 2009), and faculty engagement and buy-in are critical.

Systems/consortia can help facilitate the institutionalization strategy by proactively identifying linkages between UR and other system/consortium efforts. In particular, the system/consortium community should not see or perceive UR (or, for that matter, service learning, global engagement, learning communities, etc.) as a "project du jour," because this leads to "initiative fatigue." Leadership teams need to ensure that investments coming to and flowing from the system/consortium office act in synergy rather than in silos.

Not all investments are costly, either at the system/consortium level or at the institutional level. In fact, our experience in working with over 450 campuses is that most strategies to institutionalize UR, particularly in the early stages, are no cost or low cost. Moreover, when campuses invest the time and effort in serious analysis and dialogue, there's much economy to be realized in the size and scope of their curricula (Osborn & Paul, 2010; Paul, 2012) as well as their academic and administrative programs (Dickeson, 2010) that can then be reallocated for strategic priorities. Finally, when UR itself is viewed as an investment and not as an expense, and it is synergistically linked to enrollment management efforts as is occurring in PASSHE (Chapter 6 of this volume), this investment can lead to increases in student retention, success, and completion, as well as more revenue. As such, the return on investment is manyfold and spans the entire system.

Investing in Sustained Change.   To achieve enduring change that is sustained over the long term, systems/consortia need to invest in developing structures/groups that have responsibility for UR, communication mechanisms, and political will. Benchmarks for assessing both the change effort and the most salient outcomes need to be established and need to fit within each system/consortium in ways that link to the system/consortium strengths.

With many demands on faculty time, as well as turnover among faculty, leadership teams, and administrators, how can member campuses and the whole system/consortium maintain momentum in their efforts to scale up and institutionalize UR? As noted earlier, one strategy that can be particularly effective for protecting institutional memory and leveraging UR implementation is the establishment of some type of central campus office devoted to UR. Each campus office, through its director or coordinator, then maintains regular communication and contact with the leadership team at the central system/consortium office (which has been developed and empowered as discussed earlier) and with their counterparts at other member campuses. Several of the six systems/consortia profiled in this volume have created such a network, and they hold regularly scheduled meetings via teleconference or webconference, as well as meeting in person at statewide or system-wide events.

In addition to coordinating communication and facilitating connections among the UR leaders at the member campuses, the leadership team at the central system/consortium office should play a paramount role in ensuring that UR remains a priority discussion item for the system/consortium and institutional leaders. This can be accomplished by ensuring that agenda items are included on the regularly scheduled system/consortium meetings of key leadership groups (i.e., presidents, chief academic officers, chief financial officers, etc.).

Finally, while acquiring more knowledge about UR and initiating/funding focused projects and events are certainly essential, these will not be sufficient to realize the type of sustained change that is needed. What is needed just as much, and even more, is political will—taking the steps required to resolve practical problems of organization, communication, mobilization, and resource allocation. The search for more and better information should not be allowed to become a substitute for, or a diversion from, the harder tasks of mobilizing faculty opinion, as well as persuading faculty, administrators, development offices, and governing boards of the transformative power of UR.

References

Carstens, L., & Howell, J. (2012). Questions that matter: Using inquiry-guided faculty development to create an inquiry-guided learning curriculum. In V. S. Lee (Ed.), *New Directions for Teaching and Learning: No. 129. Inquiry-guided learning* (pp. 51–59). San Francisco, CA: Jossey-Bass.

Dickeson, R. C. (2010). *Prioritizing academic programs and services: Reallocating resources to achieve strategic balance, revised and updated.* San Francisco, CA: Jossey-Bass.

Eckel, P., Green, M., & Hill, B. (2001). *On change V, riding the waves of change: Insights from transforming institutions.* Washington, DC: American Council on Education.

Eckel, P., Green, M., Hill, B., & Mallon, W. (1999). *On change III, taking charge of change: A primer for colleges and universities.* Washington, DC: American Council on Education. Retrieved from http://www.uky.edu/Provost/APFA/Department_Chairs/on-changeIII.pdf

Frost, S. H., & Jean, P. M. (2003). Bridging the disciplines: Interdisciplinary discourse and faculty scholarship. *The Journal of Higher Education, 74,* 119–149.

Henderson, C., Beach, A., & Finkelstein, N. (2011). Facilitating change in undergraduate STEM instructional practices: An analytic review of the literature. *Journal of Research in Science Teaching, 48,* 952–984.

Hensel, N. (Ed.). (2012). *Characteristics of excellence in undergraduate research (COEUR).* Washington, DC: Council on Undergraduate Research.

Hensel, N., & Paul, E. L. (Eds.). (2012). *Faculty support and undergraduate research: Innovations in faculty role definition, workload, and reward.* Washington, DC: Council on Undergraduate Research.

Kezar, A. (Ed.). (2009). *Rethinking leadership in a complex, multicultural, and global environment: New concepts and models for higher education.* Sterling, VA: Stylus.

Kotter, J. P. (2012). *Leading change.* Boston, MA: Harvard Business Review Press.

Kuh, G. D. (2008). *High-impact educational practices. What they are, who has access to them, and why they matter.* Washington, DC: Association of American Colleges and Universities (AAC&U).

Kuh, G. D., Kinzie, J., Schuh, J. H., Whitt, E. J., & Associates. (2005). *Student success in college: Creating conditions that matter.* San Francisco, CA: Jossey-Bass.

Kuh, G. D., & O'Donnell, K. (with case studies by S. Reed). (2013). *Ensuring quality & taking high-impact practices to scale.* Washington, DC: Association of American Colleges and Universities (AAC&U).

Lynd-Balta, E., Erklenz-Watts, M., Freeman, C., & Westbay, T. D. (2006). Professional development using an interdisciplinary learning circle: Linking pedagogical theory to practice. *Journal of College Science Teaching, 35*(4), 18–24.

Malachowski, M., Ambos, E., Karukstis, K., & Osborn, J. (2010). *Collaborative research: Transformational learning through undergraduate research: Comprehensive support for faculty, institutions, state systems and consortia* (NSF-DUE #0920275, #0920286).

Osborn, J. M., & Karukstis, K. K. (2009). The benefits of undergraduate research, scholarship, and creative activity. In M. Boyd & J. Wesemann (Eds.), *Broadening participation in undergraduate research: Fostering excellence and enhancing the impact* (pp. 41–53). Washington, DC: Council on Undergraduate Research.

Osborn, J. M., & Paul, E. L. (2010, November 11). *Moving from the periphery to the center: Faculty roles in undergraduate research*. AAC&U Network Conference on Undergraduate Research In and Across Disciplines. Retrieved from http://archive.aacu .org/pkal/documents/FacultyRolesinUndergraduateResearchPowerpoint.Durham.pdf

Paul, E. L. (2012). New directions for faculty workload models: Focusing on high-impact learning practices. In N. Hensel & E. L. Paul (Eds.), *Faculty support and undergraduate research: Innovations in faculty role definition, workload, and reward* (pp. 133–145). Washington, DC: Council on Undergraduate Research.

Senge, P. M., Kleiner, A., Roberts, C., Ross, R. B., & Smith, B. J. (1994). *The fifth discipline fieldbook: Strategies and tools for building a learning organization*. New York, NY: Doubleday.

Sunal, D. W., Hodges, J., Sunal, C. S., Whitaker, K. W., Freeman, L. W., Edwards, L., ... Odell, M. (2001). Teaching science in higher education: Faculty professional development and barriers to change. *School Science and Mathematics, 101*, 246–257.

Taplin, D. H., & Clark, H. (2012). *Theory of change basics: A primer on theory change*. Retrieved from http://www.theoryofchange.org/wp-content/uploads/toco_library /pdf/ToCBasics.pdf

MITCHELL MALACHOWSKI is a professor of chemistry at the University of San Diego and a coordinator of CUR's Institutionalizing Undergraduate Research Program.

JEFFREY M. OSBORN is the dean of the School of Science and professor of biology at The College of New Jersey, and a coordinator of CUR's Institutionalizing Undergraduate Research Program.

KERRY K. KARUKSTIS is the Ray and Mary Ingwersen Professor and chair of chemistry at Harvey Mudd College, and a coordinator of CUR's Institutionalizing Undergraduate Research Program.

ELIZABETH L. AMBOS is the executive officer of the Council on Undergraduate Research.

SHONTAY L. KINCAID is the project manager for CUR's Institutionalizing Undergraduate Research Program.

DANIEL WEILER is the founder of Daniel Weiler Associates, which has conducted the project evaluation for CUR's Institutionalizing Undergraduate Research Program.

INDEX

NEW DIRECTIONS FOR HIGHER EDUCATION

ORDER FORM SUBSCRIPTION AND SINGLE ISSUES

DISCOUNTED BACK ISSUES:

Use this form to receive 20% off all back issues of *New Directions for Higher Education*.
All single issues priced at **$23.20** (normally $29.00)

TITLE   ISSUE NO.   ISBN

_____   _____   _____

_____   _____   _____

_____   _____   _____

*Call 1-800-835-6770 or see mailing instructions below. When calling, mention the promotional code JBNND
to receive your discount. For a complete list of issues, please visit www.josseybass.com/go/ndhe*

SUBSCRIPTIONS: (1 YEAR, 4 ISSUES)

☐ New Order   ☐ Renewal

        U.S.   ☐ Individual: $89   ☐ Institutional: $335
        CANADA/MEXICO   ☐ Individual: $89   ☐ Institutional: $375
        ALL OTHERS   ☐ Individual: $113   ☐ Institutional: $409

Call 1-800-835-6770 or see mailing and pricing instructions below.
Online subscriptions are available at www.onlinelibrary.wiley.com

ORDER TOTALS:

       Issue / Subscription Amount: $ _____

                Shipping Amount: $ _____
(for single issues only – subscription prices include shipping)

                 Total Amount: $ _____

SHIPPING CHARGES:	
First Item	$6.00
Each Add'l Item	$2.00

*(No sales tax for U.S. subscriptions. Canadian residents, add GST for subscription orders. Individual rate subscriptions must
be paid by personal check or credit card. Individual rate subscriptions may not be resold as library copies.)*

BILLING & SHIPPING INFORMATION:

☐ **PAYMENT ENCLOSED:** *(U.S. check or money order only. All payments must be in U.S. dollars.)*

☐ **CREDIT CARD:**   ☐ VISA   ☐ MC   ☐ AMEX

     Card number _____ Exp. Date _____

     Card Holder Name_____ Card Issue # _____

     Signature _____ Day Phone_____

☐ **BILL ME:** *(U.S. institutional orders only. Purchase order required.)*

     Purchase order # _____
                Federal Tax ID 13559302 • GST 89102-8052

Name_____

Address_____

Phone_____ E-mail_____

Copy or detach page and send to: **John Wiley & Sons, One Montgomery Street, Suite 1000,
San Francisco, CA 94104-4594**

Order Form can also be faxed to: **888-481-2665**

                                                     PROMO JBNND